A Hamburger in a Gallery

SELECTED BOOKS BY STUART ROSS

Further Confessions of a Small Press Racketeer (Anvil Press, 2015)
Our Days in Vaudeville (Mansfield Press, 2013)
You Exist. Details Follow. (Anvil Press, 2012)
Snowball, Dragonfly, Jew (ECW Press, 2011)
Buying Cigarettes for the Dog (Freehand Books, 2009)
Dead Cars in Managua (DC Books, 2008)
I Cut My Finger (Anvil Press, 2007)
Confessions of a Small Press Racketeer (Anvil Press, 2005)
Hey, Crumbling Balcony! Poems New & Selected (ECW Press, 2003)
Razovsky at Peace (ECW Press, 2001)
Farmer Gloomy's New Hybrid (ECW Press, 1999)
Henry Kafka & Other Stories (The Mercury Press, 1997)
The Inspiration Cha-Cha (ECW Press, 1996)
The Mud Game (w/ Gary Barwin, The Mercury Press, 1995)
The Pig Sleeps (w/ Mark Laba, Contra Mundo Books, 1993)
Guided Missiles (Proper Tales Press, 1990)
Smothered (Contra Mundo Press, 1990)
Wooden Rooster (Proper Tales Press, 1986)
Father, the Cowboys Are Ready to Come Down from the Attic (Proper Tales Press, 1982)
Bad Glamour (Proper Tales Press, 1980)
He Counted His Fingers, He Counted His Toes (Proper Tales Press, 1979)

TRANSLATIONS

My Planet of Kites, by Marie-Ève Comtois (trans. w/ Michelle Winters, Mansfield Press, 2015)

STUART ROSS

A Hamburger in a Gallery

LIVRES DC BOOKS

Cover art by Katy Lemay.
Author photograph courtesy of the author.
Book designed and typeset by Primeau Barey, Montreal.
Edited by Jason Camlot.

Legal Deposit, Bibliothèque et Archives nationales du Québec
and Library and Archives Canada, 1st trimester, 2015.

Library and Archives Canada Cataloguing in Publication
Ross, Stuart, author
A hamburger in a gallery/Stuart Ross.
Includes index.
Poems.
ISBN 978-1-927599-34-1 (bound).
ISBN 978-1-927599-33-4 (paperback)
1. Title.
PS8585.0841H36 2015 C811'.54 C2015-901455-7

For our publishing activities, DC Books gratefully acknowledges the financial support of the Canada Council for the Arts, of SODEC, and of the Government of Canada through Canadian Heritage and the Canada Book Fund.

Canada Council for the Arts
Conseil des Arts du Canada
Société de développement des entreprises culturelles Québec

Printed and bound in Canada.
Interior pages printed on FSC® certified environmentally responsible paper.
Distributed by Fitzhenry and Whiteside.

FSC www.fsc.org RECYCLED Paper made from recycled material FSC® C095263

DC Books
PO Box 666, Station Saint-Laurent
Montreal, Quebec H4L 4V9
www.dcbooks.ca

I am the government on the moon and
I mean to let you forgive me.

–Emily Pettit, "How to Recognize
When You Have Behaved Badly and
Behave Better"

Everyone ordering hamburgers
with a napkin in his or her lap
works for the government.

–Sommer Browning, "Federal Holiday"

CONTENTS

Duringations

Dick TV

Wychcrest Avenue

ONE EYE

Alice Notley
wrote a poem about
Robert Creeley
having only one eye.
I wrote a poem
about Alice Notley
writing a poem
about Robert Creeley
having only one eye.
I called it "One Eye."

TRANSLUS
HIONS

POEM AFTER YU JIAN

Pogo stick bursts from trees, chasing wheelchair
Commercial   Sailing elephant chops televisions, paints a dove
Campground duels with Malibu porn set   William Carlos Williams
We walk across the lawn, repair the TV antenna
Bicycle into an accordion   wander into anonymity
My neighbours have good sideburns   I'm learning a trick involving
a pineapple
The Beatles and Paul Anka ski into my house
The twins caress the dove–joy cluster
An airplane tangled in telephone wire blows up

In a simpler life we drink from the well
In a simpler life we are inundated by guests
In a simpler life the bunny leaps out of the washing machine

AND BOING

after Robert Walser's "Und Ging"

The swinger leased the shiny shack
and boing! he became a wanderer.
The blathering rabbi was a democratic bomb
and boing! he became a rawhide vegetable.
See the tilt of a landlocked garden toward Australia,
and boing! you're the king of the world.
It's nightlight applause and a turtle,
and boing! it becomes a leaden hearse.
The psycho dachshund lifts his hurt snout
and boing! he has become the Arms of Man.

MORNING FARMER

after "Grauer Morgen," by Ted Berrigan

Reagan
great needer
drawing from a harem
Fun!
drinking an icy can of gushy words
                    die, Reagan
                    a fallen
                    humping
                    trophy
                    God, you're mad in the head

POTATO PAJAMA

after a poem by Novica Tadic

Heavy kopeks asphyxiate Nehemia
Charly Lopez agrees
Morph
Banana sees a vroom New York Kentucky
Mama notates bone
Cuckoo Nana and Commander Ha-Ha
Kopeks unite herobitch

Potato pajama, yeah
has American cacophony
in Obamaville
cow angina
has come away toboggan coffee
campfire breath

THE GENTLEMANLY IMPERFECTION

after Nicanor Parra

Only the parachute of 200 waterfalls
Detains Jimmy Durante in a tuba.
Ella Fitzgerald visits a rigorous white man.

The poor river sins, servicing a toe.
Yo-Yo Ma absconds with the detritus of Ann Landers.

Me enters the twisted nova,
A dizzy male in his father's tuba.
The gentlemanly imperfection
Says doodle-doo and leers at revolutionary isms.

ANOTHER POEM AFTER YU JIAN

He's berserk.
He throws his computer into the tree.
Don Quixote slices open the box.
Everybody on earth balances planks on their heads.

The Navy haircut makes him look conventional around the dynamite.
But his caged bird dies.
He runs and runs and runs.   He runs into the alligator's jaw.

Seriously – an eye for an eye.
You cannot hide in a tent in the forest – come back.
I will embrace your computer in the bisected box.
You will comb your daughter's hair till the music begins.

ANGRY FORESTER

after Niels Hav

Angry forester/dumb & blind
kisses his size-10 slippers

Detective No-Photos-Please faults the hot opera
out-guilting the Hospital King

The slim, vacuous heaver vacates his own blood
and doodles upon his seven toes –

Frau Vindaloo is certainly lonesome, eh?
She denies the counterfeiters and the traffickers

TIERS OF SOILED TEARS

after "Tears, Oily Tears..." by James Schuyler

Cryogenics, come hop with me.
In the mustard mine, unions employ
transmogrification
heads line up in the dairy noose
snogging sufficient sheep
there's Montgomery Clift and now he's gone.
Furtive bowlers out-peep snorting orderlies
Seuss on a camel
spurting bushes laying eggs
Feargal Sharkey lunges at the fruit station
cry
and yodel
Soupy Louis' wurst and grey booty
Relocate two tiers,
slingshot like Eddie Coyle
Hanover roiled a wind-up groupie

A GUIDE TO BETTE R LIVING

24/3/12: A CENTO

And that was the last time
I would refuse
to see her as she saw herself.
A liquid golden octopus
I shall keep to myself.
Although we share a minimal
ripped shirt
I am truly horribly upset because Marilyn
put them all to sleep.
They all died
The other night at dinner   when you said
I'm waiting for my answer
in an ocean you've had to construct.

CURTAINS

I pull back the curtains. A parking lot. In the distance,
a camel wanders. The sky is nearly white with clouds.
Oil stains.

I pull back the curtains. The trees are so close together they
appear to be hugging. Caterpillars dangle between them.
The colours smudge and blur, like water coolers.

I pull back the curtains. A perfectly groomed lawn with
a folding chair in the centre. A child with Peter Ustinov's
head sits completely still. A lawnmower passes from one
side of the lawn to the other.

I pull back the curtains. Another lawn. Green, but speckled
with yellow dandelions. A rippling breeze.

I pull back the curtains. A conveyor belt carries dolls' heads
from right to left. When the heads reach the end, they fall
off the belt.

I pull back the curtains. They pull themselves closed again.

GUIDE TO BETTER LIVING: 1

Never nail a bathrobe to a train Never
tap impatiently on a window when it's
raining blood Never name a tomcat Prince
Vanilla Never store marbles in your ears

Never crawl silently through the halls
of an elementary school in the middle
of the night Never cross your fingers
in the mud Never fill your head

with good ideas or anyone else's
head Never testify against your
stapler Never ask a barber to open
a bottle of wine Never place your

open palm against the open palm
that I have designated as mine.

THIS MEANS: A CENTO

no questions asked.
I think this means:
I watched you die,
pressed to a
tooth before bed.
Oh, magic,
I walk
into the earth
with a criminal's head.
I no longer recognize myself in the
clinks on the floorboards.
Bills pile up
by the mouthful.

THE WINDOW

i

A moth against the window
likes the sensation
of glass against wings.

ii

A moth against the window
means you will soon come into
a lot of money, then lose it.

iii

A moth against the window
holds up a sign:
it is being held hostage
by the outdoors.

PERHAPS A CENTO

One paradox we weary of–
They don't make rocks like us anymore.
But I face the ice this year
In an old suit, greasy shirt and tie,
wires crossed, and history
in mint condition, and nine
door frames, warnings written
on this loveless damp winter day.
I have only what I remember
of my own voice
I've never felt so wide awake
don't worry.

ABECEDARIUM APOLOGY

I'm sorry, albumen, cherished part of the egg.
I'm sorry, Bob Crane, and the coffee table that smashed
  your head.
I'm sorry, Cannonball Adderley, I poured shampoo down
  your saxophone.
I'm sorry, Dick Sargent, that I preferred Dick York.
I'm sorry, electric eel, for your inability to spell.
I'm sorry, fistful of dollars I spent on bad poetry.
I'm sorry, galloping three-legged dog, for the inferior treats
  I fed you.
I'm sorry, halibut, Helvetica and Uncle Harry.
I'm sorry, Isabel met an enormous bear.
I'm sorry, Jonathan Winters and Suzanne Somers.
I'm sorry, koi, that you are strictly ornamental.
I'm sorry, lost emotion, lost car keys and lost opportunities.
I'm sorry, Mary Stewart and Mary Stuart Masterson.
I'm sorry, narwhal, that I signed my name to a book
  you wrote.
I'm sorry, Owen, for all that is not fair.
I'm sorry, plastic plantation and the plastic cradles
  you grow.
I'm sorry, Quincy Jones, that I ripped up your music.
I'm sorry, Rufus, dog of my childhood, and the car that ran
  you over.
I'm sorry, salivating banker in the burnt-out shell of a
  strip mall.
I'm sorry, tank of contentedly lobotomized lobsters.
I'm sorry, Uncle Harry (again), Uncle Sol and Uncle Percy.
I'm sorry, Victor Mature and the piebald horse you rode
  in on.

I'm sorry, whispered apology.
I'm sorry, Xaviera Hollander, for not buying your
board game.
I'm sorry, young anarchist in the doughnut shop
near Bessarion.
I'm sorry, Zalman Nehemiah Razovsky, for the blandness
of my name.

TRIPTYCH

i

Rivers see saliva
No sky
No dodo
Rivers bang fever
bang drifting ghost
Rain is saliva
No rain is saliva

ii

You see no rivers
banging bed birds
reading everything
drifting eyes
ghosts mirror
mirroring no river

iii

Is fever
Is sky
Is eyes

Is eyes is ghosts?
Is sky is mirrors?
Is fever is fever?

Everything is fever
Everything is sky
Everything is eyes

CENTO FOR LYNN

he begged for mercy.
far from my light house
soaked in perfume, waiting
and marking the days.

I sensed that things were
an eagle on my shoulder. pouring
through me, as truth.
I meant to write. I think of you often.

his soul falls wheezing on
tar pits, sunken repositories – entire continents.
I embrace the pillows and sheets
protected in self-ice.

the night's rich flannel sleeves.
over the street, the trees.

GUIDE TO BETTER LIVING: 2

Never press your clean-shaven
cheeks into the dewy blades of
grass that reach from the lawn
of the boy who bullied you

back in Grade 2 (his name was
Todd) when the knife-sharpener's
wife lies in her bed the mattress
thin her sons clutching her hands the

doctor standing in the shadowed
corner and pine needles brushing
against the window and outside
an ice cream truck with a flat

rolls by *bump bump bump* and
children without eyelids play in the sand.

CONFETTI CENTO

I was born, yes.
But we are not unalike.
One day we'll come loose from everything.

THE MIRROR

Their eyes followed the ball's trajectory.
Their eyes were ringed with black.
Their eyes never blinked. Not once.
Their eyes pulled covered wagons through the street.
Their eyes eclipsed their noses.
Their eyes took in the beach, the ocean, the waving hands
of a drowning man.
Their eyes went in and out of focus.
Their eyes exchanged colours.
Their eyes popped out of a car window.
Their eyes played softball against the eyes of potatoes.
Their eyes played tricks on their beleaguered mouths.
Their eyes peered around the corner, and around the corner
beyond that one.
Their eyes were the eyes that were closed in the mirror.

BETWIXTIO
NS

THE SUN

after Stuart Ross after Georg Trakl

The clouds trail behind, confused.
Each movement is silent in the leaves.
His father is dead and cannot tell him.

The pond is striped like a cartoon convict.
This is called breathing.
It scoops a flounder from the depths.

Oh throbbing cobs, quivering ears.
It can eat the earth, but chooses not to.
Time passes, then comes to a halt, outside of the frame.

THE HILL

after Mark Strand

The legs sprout from my groin,
missing the clouds the planes crawl through,
but not at the same time.
I stick a flag in the soil.

The hill never shuts up.
Like one of those fucking snakes,
I have nothing to add.
I'll send everything a postcard.

Each hour looks like the hour before.
My brain cannot contain a year.
Everything is black and white.
This is the place I'll die.

EVERYBODY HAD LOST TRACK OF TIME

after Charles Simic

A dead moth drifts in a breeze.
It limps through the streets, sputtering gas,
Holds a coconut in her arms.
She can almost hear the voice of her dead husband.

Picking dill seeds from between his teeth.
Painting a portrait of her toilet.
Had an extra shoulder that everyone mocked.
But the clouds preferred to be alone.

Up the steep hill to the cemetery
Where he'd buried his pet dog
With his neighbour's garden hose.
It was the happiest day of his life.

THE HILL

after Mark Strand

I have three of them, sometimes four,
missing the always receding steps of the escalator,
the way I was taught.
I'm incapable of acting otherwise.

The hill can do what it wants.
The skeleton of last year's squirrel.
I don't really care. I go on.
And the everything shrinks till it fits in a mailbox.

A mosquito perches on my nose, excavates.
I stand in a tiny mountain of desiccated mosquitoes.
The moon sucks the air from the air.
I'm incapable of acting otherwise.

THE REMAINS

after Mark Strand

Keys are strewn on the ground, and crumpled receipts.
When my back is turned, they will walk away.
When I am asleep, the clocks turn me back.
I am the child in clam diggers clutching a book.

They punch their cards and leave.
I recite my grandparents' names.
They tumble and jump in the leaves.
My bed holds only me now.

They dust off their skirts
By opening my mouth.
I change my shirt.
I sit in a chair and wait.

HOW PLEASANT IT IS

after Alice Burdick

The church is built of decaying books.
The bodies are built of concrete.

The corpses' fingers hover over the button
in a way that angers us.
We haven't had enough.

Clouds are glued to the sky
and the ground is dense with bankers.
They squirm across the low black ceiling,
feel the air torch their brittle skin.

Everything gets mowed flat.

IN A FOREST OF WHISPERS

after Charles Simic

I

I stagger in my living room
wedged between the piano keys
You could go cryogenic
outside your own borders

Broken toys scattered on the lawn
are bent over by coughs
Two heads and a revolver
sit and wait

Even the worms go mad
teetering on a leaf
their six legs braced
poking out my little ant mouth

II

Every time I grow a thorax
wind chimes slap my face
You could eat mouldy baseballs
at the prime minister's table

How many lawn mowers per centipede?
The river chokes on itself
coughs and splutters
curls up by the forest

People stare at me in the grocery
I pick nits out of the celery
A car drives down the aisle
You can't count its legs

III

I stain my lizard
wedded between the phytoplankton kettle
You could gnaw crustaceans
outside your own booze cans

Broken tracheae, scavenged on the law clerk,
are bequeathed by cotton grass
Two H-bombs and a revolt
syphon and wail

Even the worrywart's job
telecasting on a leading question
Their six legal holidays
poised on my little anorexia mousetrap

A HAMBURGE R IN A GALLERY

EARNING MY NOBEL PRIZE FOR LITERATURE

I have invented a new dental floss
that makes you depressed.
It will be a good seller, Dad.

Every time a car goes by my window,
my dog reads another George Eliot novel.
I will buy her a new bookmark.

Let's move on to the issue of "size."
The latest issue of *Vogue*
is bigger than the town I live in.

Mark Laba once lived a block away
and I thought that was far.
Now he lives in Vancouver.

I worry that the dog is bored.
I train her to ride a tricycle
and invent a dental floss for dogs.

Have I won
the Nobel Prize
for Literature yet?

STUDY 19

I have made paintings. I painted them.
Have you seen the horse one? It doesn't exist.
Art is of value. Governments are elected.
I finger-painted. Mother cleansed my fingers.

A man made a giant hamburger. A hamburger is in a gallery.
I washed the paint off the floor. The paint lingers.
Dogs are good at billiards. Children dance with big eyes.
You sleep. A blue jay tugs at your sleeping hair.

You painted your room. It filled with singers.
Capitalism is flawed. I entered your room.
The painting is called "Study 19." It got advertised.

SHOES ARE NOT CLOTHES

This is a skirt.
This is a bicycle.
This is a copy of *Death in Venice.*

I can't see the chalkboard.
I can't find any chalk.
How do you spell "flem"?

I'm uncomfortable naked.
I'm off balance on one foot.
I have three sisters named Tizi.

The riot took place in the square.
Eighty-four were arrested.
They are unaccounted for.

Shoes are not clothes.
I am not Thomas Mann.

Please clothes the window.
I mean please close the window.

THE ONLY SYNAGOGUE

A falcon burst out of the roiling cloud.
We repressed a desire to pray.
Days of silence passed, then
Tootsie asked Bill about his grandfather.
"He was a learned man," said Bill, "but
he smoked too much near the gas pump."
Bill modelled his grandfather's tefillin.
We looked at each other and shrugged,
after which we crept down darkened streets.
Larry offered us use of his rec room.
It was the only synagogue in town.
The congregation was always
pinching the bagel and shooting the breeze.
The postman said he was adept at
scooping the fish and hugging the cloud.

ALEKHINE VS BOGOLJUBOV 1

The text is based
on the idea of
answering stenographically
with orchestra pits
(instead of the more
usual trapdoors and bells).
The text is interesting
innovation which gives
new life to this
variation. The text
parries all of the
supermarket's threats
in a remarkably simple
manner. The text
stops a young ambulance crew
on a ready-mix truck
at gravity's 30th
paragraph. In the long run,
this must lose
at least a red monster.
A hard game!

FOURTET

1. A finger pressed against the spines of a cactus. The science teacher, close to retirement, will find his wife gone when he gets home. The cafeteria no longer offers the children potato chips or chocolate bars.

2. The odor from the creek. A torn dog collar. The moon's weak glow. A car rolls out of its pebble driveway, unaware of the driver within it. The quivering nose of a raccoon.

3. Why watch the television? Who put the newspaper on the picnic table? The can of peas, open. An airplane. In the lobby of the Day's Inn, a man named Tom collapses.

4. They stood in a line, shifting from foot to foot, glancing at one another, each waiting for someone else to begin.

MY LIFE DURING A CERTAIN PERIOD

I ate crow. I flew directly.
My foot hit a treetop. I hit my foot.
Altitude? The Rosens' TV antenna.
I landed Tuesday. Wednesday I slept.
My teacher phoned. I was an asset to the class.
I jumped off things. Flight was gone.
I turned to needlepoint. Night arrived.
An election. Nothing changed.
TV was good. I watched TV.

ONE-LINE POEMS

DOLPHINS

There is intelligence in the water.

ICE CUBES

Put something square in your round drink.

BOOKMOBILES

I read the same book as a person in another small town.

THE MOVIE LINE-UP

Everybody wants to see what everyone's seeing.

SIXTIES SITCOM

Keep William Windom employed.

SONNET

Bye Bye Birdie.
Going Down the Road.
The Ticket That Exploded.
Al Purdy.

Felix the Cat.
Dennis Kucinich.
A Day in the Life of Ivan Denisovich.
Doctor Rat.

Welcome to the Monkey House.
Evelyn Lau.
I Can See Clearly Now.
Mickey Mouse.

Jack and the Beanstalk.
Talk Talk.

ALEKHINE VS BOGOLJUBOV 2

The first match.
The complications.
The idea of fixing.

The natural support.
The force of the move.
The following fine.

A satisfactory game.
An interesting continuation.
A winning position.

A last desperate swindle.

THREE STORIES

1.

A swimming pool, empty. Dead leaves. Moira pulls open the drapes, just a little. An ice cream truck. A drumroll of footsteps.

2.

Wind hits the brick wall. A television antenna. Meanwhile, the governor's phone call doesn't come. A taxi stuck in traffic. Who bought the last newspaper?

3.

A siren. Later, Mother fries up macaroni. The lottery numbers. Geography. Physics. Home economics. The man leaps off his bed. He bathes.

SONNET

Stranger in a Strange Land.
The Bonzo Doo Dah Dog Band.
A Raisin in the Sun.
Attila the Hun.
Preston Sturges.
Anthony Burgess.

My Favorite Martian.
Johnny Carson.
Mama Told Me Not to Come.
Eve Plumb.
Wislaw Szymborska.
Federico García Lorca.

Cagney and Lacey.
John Wayne Gacy.

SEVEN NEW DENVER POEMS

Black spider
scurries on pebble beach.
So many choices!

*

Waves lap
against beach.
The sound
of applause
in an empty
stadium.

*

Shard
of green glass
carried on
the shoulders
of grey
and white
pebbles.

*

Valhalla Glacier
crouches behind
the mountains
waiting
for
its close-up.

*

Detergent bottle
bobs
on the choppy
water –
nothing
to clean.

*

Clouds
of grey cotton
polish
the mountaintops.

*

Beckham
steps onto the
log I'm sitting on.
My pencil
slips.

THREE LEASHES

It is winter. A water dish holds a dead fly.
The dog is Rufus. The dog is Lily.
I bought three leashes. She chewed them up.
I read her Jack London. She tilted her head.

An intruder passes by. An intruder passes.
The mail arrives. Nothing handwritten.
I kissed Rufus on the lips. He called me a fag.
He didn't. Dogs don't speak English.

Dogs don't speak. Dogs feel no remorse.
I am filled with remorse. I eat a burger.
I declined the fries. The Coke was refillable.
Lily needs to run. The lake contains waves.

A car runs out of gas. Rufus sits by the grave.
An intruder walks by. Everything smells.
She offers a paw. The treat is withheld.
The room becomes dark. He sleeps in a circle.

SONNET

First Men in the Moon.
96 Tears.
Daniel Boone.
Tears for Fears.

The Trouble with Harry.
Peter O'Toole.
Leisuresuit Larry.
Don't Be Cruel.

The Barber of Seville.
Mario Lanza.
Mink DeVille.
Tony Danza.

The Harder They Fall.
Nelson Ball.

THE RAVINE

Is there anything
in the ravine

that was in the ravine
when I was there

forty-six years
ago?

TERRIBLE MEN WHO LOVED TO DANCE

They snatch the limping deer
from the side of the muddy road,
throw it into the back of their pickup.
The mountain shimmies into
a wispy gown of August clouds
and waits for its date. A road
goes round and round,
the strap of a sandal climbing
Melina Mercouri's slender calf,
and facts like cigarette butts
pepper the lake's quiet surface. At
the Silverton Country Inn, the jukebox
unfolds like magnolia petals
and thereupon step men with
blood and bad ideas
smeared across
their crystal cheeks.

TARJETAS POSTALES

for Anne Waldman

BAÑOS, ECUADOR

Swimming pool carved into a mountain.
The water, her *termales,* the beachball of flesh.
¡O what incomparable medicinal value!

L'HÔTEL DE VILLE, PARIS

She pushes me into the mirror.
Everyone wears black: a sack on a cart.
At the break, 200 lbs.

AGHIA GALINI, GREECE

The boat is a dog on a leash.
The houses the toenails of the mountains.
I'm not complaining.

HÀ NÔI, VIETNAM

Landscape of the one-pillar pagoda.
Three women on bench, red basket on wall.
The sky, blue, tolerates all.

GEORGETOWN, BAHAMAS

The dragon cloud lunges for the beach.
The cost is 40 cents.
We miss you ever more.

DURINGATI ONS

LESION OF SUPERHEROES

Oh surly Gene Kelly
fondling dead hands
like a sweet choo-choo
like an all-American
potato. Gene Kelly
I kiss your leprous feet.
The aching movie sashays
up my arms, my neck
and onto my loving cheeks.
They explode like a kid
on a slide, drinking blurry
martinis.

                    I will teach you
a dance I invented
six seconds ago. An airplane
will put you on its knee,
transport you to a sparrow-
filled stage. Look at
the endless line of dancers.
Look at Ford Madox Ford
kill or kiss Gene Kelly, or,
more specifically, Gene Kelly's
windshield, turning and
turning like an egg on a
lazy susan.

                    Meanwhile, I
look like a jungle of spoons.
Handsome, but broken-headed

and wordless. I'm
not kidding. After the
party, there's another
party, and another after
that, swooping like an
electric bulb, drowning
like a question mark,
an ostrich with plumage
of wheat. Imperfect
but more provocative
than a rubber band
or a wrong-buttoned
ape.

THE CONTINUING SAGA OF THE WIND

I am part of the moping mortuary.   Here is my
business card.   A man and his furniture kiss in the
sanctuary.   They intend good. I intend

                                                            a backdrop.
Did you know your eyes are the most mesmerizing
skylights?   Wag your tail. Explain the sublime.   A sunset
hit me on the head, left me among the coughing rocks
to consider math. I flunked.

                                              The wind comes in the front
door, climbs out the back window. It is cradled by the anxious sky,
which I had purchased at the supermarket that tucked me in,
singing a just-sufficient
                                        lullaby about chickens and two people
in love.   Water as clear as water stinks in the dark. It's a miracle.
A miracle is like a box we crouch in. The box is lodged in
the rubble of heaven
                                    at four in the afternoon.

A BLOB AGAINST THE POINTY MOON

We juggle not, lest
we be juggled like
the silhouette of a blob
against the pointy moon.

This grown-up water
has shores on every side,
and above, and below. I do
nothing with my nearby nostrils.

On the count of three,
as counted by a beautiful
girl, I vanish. It happens
every time. (The tree
is aware of the dog's bark.)

I will now reveal
my identity: I am
a this or that, a
thing left behind.

I teach the future the alphabet,
then wait for my wings.

TOWARDS THE FUTURE

I fumble a staccato tangerine, drifting far from us in this life of the us of us. Men forget to send their hesitant feelers into a huddle of severe and curling convicts. Nothing to be seen here! And by here, I mean inside the belly of a wooden bird that saunters down the runway, flashbulbs popping. Fantastic! I say that I stand here on two feet, but I have shoes painted on my hands, for I am interested and intelligent, a living creature, an insect, a rodent, a roiling sphere of hullabaloo. Behold: they filled the stadium with the chicken breasts of exultation, a task devised for both pleasure and torment. We move swiftly, accept hardship, hit Huckleberry Finn over the head with an oar, in case things get out of hand. We set a foot on the landscape, a featureless shape visible from a state of diminished happiness. Who has seen the breathless stock market, bursting out of its bustier, so noisy, non-existent? Men mobilize towards the future, out of control.

NORMALITY

From the town square,
we heard the clang
of paper bags. Mysterious
sores dwindled on our
foreheads, our foreheads
dwindled on the sidewalk.
The authorities noticed a
black spot on my collar.
The bus driver hung over
the hardware store, his
nose chipped, playing
Xenakis on the piano.
Heads of cauliflower
glitter in the pink
of the night sky. I'm
more normal than my
body language suggests,
more normal than
an onion boarding a bus.
Is that something I saw
on a cartoon while
sipping cream soda?
We pile into a car and
drive into the fog, our
gums beginning to bleed,

our hiccoughs choosing
the line breaks in
our poems. The publisher
kicks us out of her office.
We have killed the English
language. Dark clouds
rain empty tin cans
on what's left of
Toronto. We apply
for several credit cards.

THE SKATERS

I.

Some funny dogs play tambourine,
rapturous as an autopsy
performed in a girdle. Their bold friends
of yesterday lick each other's cheeks
beneath the shadow of snowy evergreens.
So much snow in the pig cathedrals
that drift across the winter sea.
I come clean: I saw you in the news.
You were moving around in a great
horizontal wind. The military police
stuck words on your motion squiggles.
You became unborn. Tragedy invaded.
The piano sagged beneath the weight
of the question. Each flake
dissolved until you could go out
into it, your teeth in your
old-fashioned pocket. Schubert
wore shoes, but mostly for
publicity purposes. He drifted over
the horizon in a flock of balloons.
I could barely stand it. I held
him in my hand. I looked for him
in hot and cold. I found him
in you, you tiny speck.

II.

The judge has been
dead for twenty-six
years, the courthouse
destroyed by a happy
earthquake. He listens
to your motion squiggle
right by the jury's glazed eyes,
then dissolves into the glittering
shadows of the unborn. Outside,
in the empty street, a stack
of girdles, teetering in the morning
breeze, overthrows the municipal
government. I see you stop
in midsentence, the winter
icequakes rumbling under the sea.
You drop to your hands
and knees, and examine
a tiny speck of
the shooting of the husband
of the woman in
the baby carriage.

III.

I looked for him beneath the shadows
that drift across each flake.
In the pig cathedrals, in hot and cold,
the piano sagged, dissolved until
he drifted over so much snow
you became unborn. I came clean, I saw you
rapturous, your teeth in your
horizontal wind. You were moving around
as an autopsy; a flock of balloons
stuck words on your old-fashioned pocket.
The military police wore shoes,
performed in a girdle, but mostly for
some funny dogs. I could barely
play tambourine, him in my hand,
in you, each other's cheeks.
The winter sea of yesterday licked
you in the news, motion squiggles
beneath the weight. Tragedy invaded.
I held their bold friends into it.
I found him, Schubert, you tiny speck
of snowy evergreens.

POEM DURING A TALK BY CARLA HARRYMAN

We are not happy
until we are almost
noise. To make noise,
the Viet Nam war
is focused on
improvisation, mingled
with kind notes
and protective armour.
Anais Nin is quieted,
then she engages in
new ways to emerge
out of shapelessness.
No one notices
the above statement.
Someone else keeps
opening up André Breton
in the hospital,
as if out of nowhere.
A gifted composer
was lost, criticizing
to the point of
disintegration.
The dreamed son
paints Bush/Cheney's
headless heads.
That's a structure.

DID YOU BELIEVE ME?

Have you seen the boulevard?
The waffle? The rain?
It's tough to be automated,
to sit on the wooden bench
at a stoplight and hold
on to the trees. The trees
repeat into the distance.
At the end is a banquet
and the sound of a piano,
a black and white bird,
startled and wrapped in plastic.
I'm just kidding. Did you
believe me? I emerged from
the Norton Anthology and
learned how to breathe,
how to freckle the paint,
how to identify a noun
in a crate of soft drinks.
A horse taught an enthusiastic
class on how to snort.
He spiraled through his
automated language, his
tail stretching to the horizon,
several blocks away. He had
only recently left the sanatorium.
Children played with a forest
in a bookstore that specialized
in graffiti.

LOVE

Civilization, though distant,
keeps a diary. The diary
is missing.
Let's attend a concert.
Because we're thirsty
and unbalanced, rumbling
amid the suspicious
ideas that scratch
our bodies, the wilting
truckers who wag
through life with
a certainty of *knowing.*
I met you in the detritus;
we held paintbrushes
as if we were holy. We
were ruled by rules,
yet the sky complains
about its dentures,
the fact that it
doesn't fit in. Love
kills trouble, promotes
clarity, lays the head
of a delicate landscape
in its quivering lap.

BUILDINGS, WINTER

What is frozen in the road?
Who has castrated Bill?
A saleswoman danced
on a giant turntable,
on the surface of the glistening
sun. Did I say sun?
Where is the egg?
Who plunged the spatula
into the gloom?
The nurse has saved several buildings
like I told her to.

CONFETTI

I tell you:
I am unwilling
to unbend my legs.

I have other priorities.
Por ejemplo, I am
mild-mannered.

I present my neighbours
with a broken pretzel.

DIC
K TV

DICK TV

after Tom Clark

And the television! And the television! And the television!
Plus the face of Dick Cheney!
The guts inside his head on the television screen!
Wake up in a tent, Dick Cheney! Buried to your neck
in sand!
Wake up surrounded by those who survived
your bombs! Feel their stumps against your flesh!
Snivel at their stumps!
Your lips tremble. Sand blows in your mouth.
You squint through the television screen,
your mouth filled with sand,
your trigger finger frozen in sand,
your asshole packed with sand,
your chest immobilized by sand.
You are a sitcom, a commercial, a reality show,
a music video, a news clip, a cop show,
the Smothers Brothers, *My Favorite Martian,*
My Mother the Car, Mr. Ed,
The Ghost and Mrs. Muir, Flip Wilson Flip Wilson
Flip Wilson.
You are the silence between commercials.
A white subtitle against a snow-blown landscape.

MELOPHANOLOGO

The doorknob considers its qualities: the hand, the turn.

Outside, leaves leaf through leaves of Philip Levine,

while, inside, a porcelain mug shatters on the kitchen table.

An earlobe bleeds; drops hit the linoleum floor.

Consciousness is only the memory of consciousness.

Ring! Hello? Ring! Hello? Ring! Hello?

FAST FOOD

12:07 p.m.
The burger is dropped into the oil.
It bobs. It is dead meat.

12:09 p.m.
The condiments are squeezed onto the bun.
O Jackson Pollock.

12:10 p.m.
He wraps the meal in yellow paper
and slides it across the blue counter.

12:23 p.m.
She crumples the yellow paper
into a ball, wipes her mouth on her sleeve.

12:24 p.m.
Her cellphone dances across the table.
Her mother's been rushed to the hospital.
Rain starts to fall.

12:53 p.m.
She is too late.
Her father sobs into the palm
of his right hand.

1:01 p.m.
The burger is dropped into the oil.

SELF-PORTRAIT WITH A PENNY

Did I pick up the penny?
Was I so cheap I picked up the penny?
Did I put it in my pocket?
Or spend it right away?
Can you still buy anything for a penny?
Is this 1963?
Someone told me it is fifty years later, but is she reliable?
Did she carry a bag of celery in her arms?
How many pennies do you need so you can buy an
  Archie comic?
Or buy a Dodge Dart?
Would the amount of pennies needed to buy a Dodge Dart
  fit in a Dodge Dart?
How many Dodge Darts can you fit in a phone booth?
Is that a stupid question?
Am I a cheap bastard for picking up a penny?
You know what it does to my lower back picking up
  a penny?
Have you heard of hospitals?
Ever see a hospital?
See all those people with oxygen tanks smoking cigarettes
  by the hospital door?
Do you have any cigarettes?
Would a penny change your mind?

ELEGY

Nice haircut, fiddlehead,
juggled beneath
a slobbering dog
by the side
of a gold-veined
lake.

MORE ONE-LINE POEMS

THE SOLID OCEAN

Stuck among seahorses.

LEAPING INNARDS

Something indistinct on the subway tracks.

SLEEP CRAFT FOR BEGINNERS

Pry the second eye closed.

POLITICAL POEM

This is a political poem.
Shortly I will allude
to some political things.
Not yet, though.
First: a one-winged bat
is dead on my sidewalk.
Then: the lake is crispy today.
Also: the man in the wizard gown
drove by in a Honda.
Now for the political part.
Right after I get some Triscuits.
I like them with soy cheese
and avocado. Everything
is political. "Even that piece
of chewed gum on the ground
with pebbles stuck in it?" Yes,
even that piece of chewed gum.
"So when you were saying
you were going to allude to
something political, that
was a trick, you were already
doing it." Eat the rich.

ADVENTURES IN BRUXISM

Nice temporomandibular joint you've got here.
Filled with unanswered letters from people
you care about, plus brownshirts chasing you
through synagogue hallways, and exam booklets
unfolded on the desk in front of you
and you realize you haven't attended
a class in thirty years, and besides,
you forgot to learn how to read.

                                        How flat
are your teeth? I have draped a tablecloth
across one ground molar and placed three
settings. I have invited Serge Gainsbourg,
Vanessa Paradis and Stephen Hawking,
the three people from history
I would most like to dine with
in your mouth. After a serving of
partridge with poached pear, some snooker
on an adjoining molar. If earth were
as flat as your night-ground teeth,
the sun would have less
work to do.

CRUNCH

I crunched myself into
a chair while he crunched
numbers in his office and
the family with the two-headed
– sorry, towheaded – boy
crunched on rotten sunflower seeds.
Boots crunched on the snow
outside the door, face crunching
against the frost-covered window.
In a deserted jail cell,
a cockroach crunched on an aphid
the way you crunch on a pomegranate
seed, or a pomegranate seed
crunches on you. By next Thursday,
we will have crunched the ugly
clouds into wisps of tissue
that crunch slowly into winter.

BEANS

The proofreader found an error. Towheaded for two-headed.
He put two-headed. It got printed.
He bought a falafel on the street. No onions, please.

He remembered catching onion instead of union. He cried.
He laughed because an onion made him cry. He was on a bridge.
He swung a leg over the railing. The water was red.

Soon his body would be cold. Soon he would never go home.
A friend was standing beside him. They went for toast and beans.
He asked where the beans grew. The waitress had only one ear.

ACCRETION URN

Image go floating out of my head. Land on a page. Splat. No need to eat it if you don't want to. There is little to gain in the assembly of a committee. The pleasure derived from coming to consciousness is measured against drowning in the dreams of your own report card. If you are experiencing caffeine unconsciousness, politically speaking, please place your bag on the floor in front of you and back up slowly. An officer will be glad to assist you in settling into one of our comfortable electric chesterfields. We run only in the ravines our dead friends have written about. Dollop your thoughts into a cupped cloud and curdle the cloud in your extended curved tongue. Leave your 3-D glasses in the appointed bin on your way out.

DAILY WRITING PROMPT #117

Write a
goddamn poem,
you weasel.

WYCHCREST AVENUE

WYCHCREST AVENUE

In the
mouth
of
a red dog
a green ball.

*

Rectangular
white
truck
glides through
the empty street.

*

Six conifers
confer
beneath
billowing clouds.

*

Bird shit
on red brick.

*

In the cold breeze
a peanut shell
rocks
on a rock.

*

Black squirrel,
brown railing.
Slips,
recovers.

*

Clear plastic
cigarette wrapper
struggles
amid the dry leaves.

*

In a puddle
of dead leaves,
a motorcycle
leaning.

UNT
ITLED

p
aper

eyegl
asses

praw
        n

prawn prawn
eyeglasses

paper
over
eyeglasses

over
over

paper
over

paper paper

eyeg
lasses

pretendd

sallowe'en

glod

doodledle

nett'le

WYCHCREST AVENUE II

a red dog

rectangular, white
amid the

of leaning
cold breeze

*

dry leaves
struggles

slips
amid

the empty
a puddle

*

bird six
a peanut shell
motorcycle
dead mouth

DOUBLE SONNET

First
time
swallows
off
curtains
stained cat
curses
financial
time travel.
Filters
should apply
pencils
scratch
into

linoleum
tongue dimples.
Save
cream
pavement
grooming
creased
cubicle cheese.
When you
tie
forks
you
count
lips.

THEN:

window snap

open

a worm in the mouth of the mouth of

the will

lasts   ripples

(pine)

below the cars

exhausted

grasps

torn pag

brick flutter

balcony

hat passes

over heads

under the

newspaper box:

a bat

polio

4 TINY POEMS I WROTE ON MARCH 15, 2014

On the edge
of the highway:
a giant eraser.

*

Where did it go?
What?
The piebald
dog who
invented
the stapler.

*

The air came in
the window. I
breathed it
carefully.

*

Later on,
a helicopter
collapsed
on the dance floor.

SPELLING

Since
squids
watch
blond
technicians,
storms
entertain
possibilities
forbidding
frothy
tsunamis.
Spelling
is
everyone's
downfall.
Johnny
stabs
dinner,
emphasizing
fifty
disadvantages
affecting
feet
soaked
by
Coke.

THE INT ERV IEW

Jason Camlot: So I am here with Stuart Roth, a poet of a book called *Hamburger in a Gallery* and I am going to be asking Stuart questions about his book. So, Mr. Roth, you have already published a collection of poems before, am I right?

Stuart Ross: The name is Ross, not Roth. Maybe you are thinking of Philip Roth. I'm Stuart Ross with two "s's."

JC: Stuart Rossk.
SR: Yeah, Stuart Ross, no "k" at the end, just Stuart Ross. I have had several books of poetry before this, about seven or eight.
JC: So why do you need to publish another book of poetry? Did you forgot to say something in the last one and that's why you had to do another one?
SR: That's a very good question, because with a lot of poets I wonder the same thing–why they are bothering to write another book of poetry. I am determined in each of my books of poetry to do something very different, and this, to me, is wildly different from any book I have had before, so I think it is not redundant to do this particular book.
JC: So, is it because you didn't do the other ones in the right way? Is that what you're saying?
SR: I think that in some of my books I hadn't taken big enough leaps from what I had done previously, so in a sense I didn't do some of those books right.
JC: So did you get this one right?
SR: Well, you know, you publish a book and then you question everything you have done continually for the rest of your life. For the moment it feels right for me, but I am sure I will have regrets after it is published.
JC: Okay, thank you. Who is You-Gee-Anne?
SR: Um, Yu Jian, and I am not sure how that is pronounced either.
JC: Did you know him personally?
SR: I do not know him personally.

JC: Was he your teacher?

SR: He was not my teacher, but a mentor of mine named Ron Padgett, who is one of my favourite poets, translated a book of Yu Jian's poetry. Yu Jian is a contemporary Chinese poet. In fact, Ron and Yu Jian collaborated on some poems without knowing each other's language. Ron wrote lines in English and Yu Jian wrote lines in Chinese and they got translators to translate them so they could each read what the other had written. I have never met the man, but I would love to meet him.

JC: So Ron Padgett really knows Yu Jian, but you don't know him?

SR: Yeah, that's right, I'm just a pretender.

JC: You're a pretender? So you're pretending to be Yu Jian or Ron Padgett?

SR: I'm pretending to be a guy who has the right to collaborate with the works of Yu Jian without his permission.

JC: Do you think this could get you in trouble maybe?

SR: I don't know, I guess I will find out. It's a kind of trouble I'd like to get into.

JC: Do you know Ron Padgett?

SR: I do know Ron Padgett.

JC: Is he your teacher?

SR: No, he is not my teacher, but I've learned a lot from his poetry–I've learned a ton.

JC: Okay, thank you. What's a Transloooshion?

SR: Translushions. Why did I call that section Translushions?

JC: And a related question, some of your poems say they come after other things that I can't find in your book. For example, your poem "And Boing" is said to come after Robert Walser's "Und Ging," but it doesn't come after that. Where is Robert Walser's "Und Ging"? Did you forget to include it in your book?

SR: Well, I would say that most books don't necessarily contain absolutely everything that has been written. They only contain what is currently written for that book–

JC: That would be too big of a book.
SR: Yeah, that would be too big a book...and so that poem was, in fact, written *after* Robert Walser's poem. It was written *after* both in terms of time and in terms of being in honour of...In a sense, that's what I mean by "after." Your other question was what does Translushions mean. It was four in the morning when I put this book together and I came up with these section titles and I am trying to remember why. It must be translations crossed with–
JC: Loooshions.
SR: Possibly with Lushions. Um, solutions? I will have to get back to you on that because I don't remember. They are not normal translations because I am not literally translating them and doing an English version of the poem with all the same content from the Chinese.
JC: Was Robert Walser Chinese?
SR: Nope.
JC: Does he know Yu Jian?
SR: No, I don't think Robert Walser ever met Yu Jian or Ron Padgett. Certainly not me...He was a Swiss writer who wrote in German.
JC: So does *Und Ging* mean *And Boing* in German?
SR: It does not. *Und Ging* made me think of *And Boing.*
JC: So it is just a pretend translation? What does *Und Ging* mean?
SR: It's a translushion.
JC: So that's what you mean, that it is pretending to be a translator?
SR: It is approaching translation from another way–translating from a language I don't know.
JC: So just to be clear, you didn't forget to put Robert Walser's "Und Ging" in your book?
SR: No, no, I never intended to.
JC: Okay, thank you very much. What does "Potato Pajama" mean? Is it pajamas made out of potatoes or pajamas with pictures of potatoes on them? And a related question, is there such a thing as "pajama"?

Because I always thought it was pajamas with an "s." What does a single pajama look like?

SR: I don't like to prescribe too much, so I put out this idea of "potato pajama" and readers do what they want with it. If I intended specifically for the reader to picture something in their head, it's unlikely I could make the reader picture that thing, because I don't know all the readers who read the book. So I'm happy to put something out there that is ambiguous and let the reader play with it, give them room to play. As to singular pajama vs. plural, I had never thought of that before and I don't know.

JC: It could be a pajama for people with only one arm or leg, too… I was thinking.

SR: It's possible, yeah, maybe it is.

JC: So potato pajama then means pajama made out of potatoes? For me it does, so is that the right answer?

SR: I had never thought about that. Sometimes when you write a poem, other people get to tell you what it's about later and it's really exciting to have these things explained for you. The poet doesn't have to know what everything means or what everything suggests in a poem.

JC: That's interesting. It is my pleasure. Um, on page 8, when the gentlemanly imperfection says "doodle-doo," I assume it says it in an English accent?

SR: If that's the way you hear it, you can go right ahead with that.

JC: 'Cause is "doodle-doo" a more gentlemanly way of saying "toodle-loo"?

SR: It could very well be that I was thinking of "toodle-loo" and wrote "doodle-doo" by accident. The words that were in Spanish by Nicanor Parra in the last line of his poem, whose name I forget, looked something like "doodle-doo," so that's what I went with.

JC: Do you know Nicanor Parra?

SR: I do not know Nicanor Parra, but he is still alive and 100 years old and lives in Chile. A very close friend of mine, Jim Smith, went down on a pilgrimage and met Nicanor Parra a couple of years ago.

JC: And just to be sure, because it is related to an earlier question I asked, that poem by Nicanor Parra is not supposed to be in your book?

SR: No, it wasn't intended to be in the book...

JC: In the same poem, is "doodle-doo" kind of a dirty joke? Is it really gentlemanly, this poem? I am thinking, what is a gentleman for you?

SR: It's interesting that you ask that question because the word "leers" appears in here and leering is something that is a little scandalous. So "leers" and "doodle-doo" appearing in the same line perhaps suggests something ungentlemanly. Your questions assume that I carefully consider every goddamn word in each of my poems and often I do not. The word in Spanish looked like the word "gentlemanly" and so that's why I wrote that word. And it occurs to me that "leer" in Spanish means "to read."

JC: So you were pretending to translate the poem again?

SR: I was trying to find a way of translating a poem in a language I don't know.

JC: So related to an earlier question I asked, is this kind of like a naughty poetry?

SR: No...

JC: Is Niels Hav a real person?

SR: Yes, he's a Danish poet who I have met and corresponded with.

JC: So it is not a typo?

SR: Everything about his name looks wrong for someone whose first language is English.

JC: Yeah, but you know him, so this is actually a real person?

SR: Yeah, yeah, I have a book by him and that is the name that appears on the cover. I showed him this translation and he wrote back that it was very accurate.

JC: So then...you can speak the Dutch language?

SR: I know a few words in Dutch–like *lekker* means tasty–but in fact this is Danish and I don't know any words in Danish. Niels Hav is from Denmark.

JC: I understand.

SR: I had a Dutch girlfriend once and I tried to impress her father by learning Dutch, so I learned a whole bunch of Dutch. I don't remember much anymore, but it's a great-sounding language... But I know no Danish.

JC: Have you ever eaten *Vla*? It is not in the book, it is just something that I have eaten that is from Denmark–no, from Amsterdam. It reminds me of Hav without an "e."

In "Tiers of Soiled Tears," who was nicer: Montgomery Clift or Eddie Coyle? Who was handsomer and who was the better poet? I am assuming they were poets.

SR: Neither of them are poets. Eddie Coyle is a fictitious character from a book called *The Friends of Eddie Coyle* by George V. Higgins, and I don't know why that name came to me. Montgomery Clift was an amazing actor from the late forties right up to the early sixties when he died. He was a very beautiful man, very attractive. Eddie Coyle was played in the movie version by Robert Mitchum, who is sort of handsome in a craggy way, but I think Clift is the better-looking of the two.

JC: Who is nicer?

SR: I would say that Montgomery Clift is probably nicer than Eddie Coyle.

JC: I thought so too. In the second section of your book, it offers a guide for better living, but a question occurred to me. Better than what? Do you think that better and worse are relative depending on the kind of apartment building you are living in? Do you think you're better than other people?

SR: What I mean by better living is living better than one is currently living. If you can improve the quality of your existence, hopefully this poem can help guide you. I don't think I'm better than other people and it doesn't have anything to do with whatever kind of apartment someone might live in.

JC: I understand. Some of your poems' titles begin with numbers and then a word. For instance "24/3/2: A Cento." Are the numbers code for something meaningful?

SR: Well, I don't know if many of my poems begin with numbers. That might be the only one. That would have been the date I wrote the poem, so March the twenty-fourth of 2012. That is what that is code for.

JC: Is that meaningful?

SR: Um, it's the date I wrote that poem. It's only meaningful insofar as it marks the day I wrote the poem.

JC: Why do you tell us the date you wrote that poem but not other poems in the book?

SR: What happened was, I write and I write and I write and then I often look at my poems much later. I wrote that in New Denver, B.C., during a workshop I led and I had given titles to a whole bunch of things I wrote, but not that one – but I did record the date that I wrote it. So in the absence of any other title, I just used the date as the title.

JC: Speaking of titles, what does A Cento mean? Does the title "This Means: A Cento" mean anything? And a related question, do poems mean in a deeper way than things that aren't poems?

SR: A cento is a poem in which every line comes from another poet. So I have a whole stack of books, I flip open one book, see a line I like and I write it down. I flip open another book by another poet and I steal a line and put it down. That is what a cento is; I think it's a Latin word for patchwork or quilt.

JC: Is that your translation? Is it like a pretend translation?

SR: No, it's in a book by Ron Padgett called *The Handbook of Poetic Forms*. I didn't make that up, although I may be remembering it wrong. The reason the poem is called "This Means" is because the phrase appears in the second line of the poem and I thought that was significant.

JC: Do things mean in a deeper way than things that are not poems?

SR: No, I don't think they mean in a deeper way and I don't necessarily think they mean in a different way. A poem can mean in the same way that an abstract painting can mean, or an experimental film.
JC: What about a butter knife?
SR: I think a butter knife is a butter knife, and that's what it is. You look at it and everyone looks at it and says, "That is a flipping butter knife." When they look at poems, the poems mean different things to different people, while I think a butter knife has a more objective interpretation.
JC: So is it a poem that means or is it *because* it is a poem that it means?
SR: My head is going in circles right now from that question. It's a meta-question and I can't deal with it.
JC: I don't understand that question. In the "Abacadabra" poem you say you are sorry for a lot of things. Do you feel as though you have been a bad person in your life? Are these the only things you are sorry for? What are you the *most* sorry for?
SR: It is an *Abecedarium* poem, because it goes through the alphabet. If you look here, I have Albumen, Bob Crane, Cannonball Adderley, Dick Sargent. So A, B, C, D, etc., all the way through. So this Abecedarium is one of apology and I'm not necessarily the speaker of that poem; it could be that someone else is–
JC: Is it Ron Padgett?
SR: It isn't my friend Ron Padgett; he isn't the speaker of the poem.
JC: Hav?
SR: It is not Niels Hav. I don't think it's anyone who we've come across in the book so far. It is an imaginary person and perhaps some part of me that just says, "Fuck, I apologize for every fucking thing, I apologize for everything." The thing I am most sorry for in my life is probably anytime that anyone has felt hurt in response to anything I've done. I don't know if that comes up anywhere in this poem. If it doesn't, that probably means it wasn't me talking.
JC: I think it does very strongly in "I'm sorry, tank of contentedly lobotomized lobsters."

SR: If that's the way you interpret that, I'm not going to disabuse you of it.

JC: Thank you. In "Triptych," when you say that everything is eyes in the poem, are you on acid? And as a follow-up, do you do drug poetry?

SR: I am not on acid. In the "everything is eyes" lines though…I could see why you might ask that question.

JC: I know.

SR: Ah, drug poetry, I am interpreting that as being poetry one writes while under the influence of drugs. I have never written anything while under the influence of drugs. Although I once deliberately got myself very drunk and wrote a short story and I was very pleased with it.

JC: This question refers to an earlier question that I asked before. Which is a better guide to better living: "Guide to Better Living 1" or "2"? Like, if you only had to read one to get the gist of how to live better, which one should I read?

SR: I can't help you on that. If you only read one and you luck out and read the one that will help you most, then that's great. Any individual would maybe be helped more by one than the other, or maybe just by the idea that you can live better by *not* doing something.

JC: Is that a trick question?

SR: Well, you're the one who asks the questions, so I don't know.

JC: It is. "The Mirror." In "The Mirror," whose eyes are you referring to? And is it someone special to you? Or is that too personal a question?

SR: I have always thought of it as the eyes of the same group of people each time. Their eyes were ringed with black, their eyes never blinked. It just occurred to me now, hearing your question, that it might be nice if it was a different "their" for every sentence.

JC: So because their eyes in the first line are the eyes that are following the ball's trajectory, but then their eyes in the second line…aren't those the eyes of the ball?

SR: That's a great reading of the poem. And then in the third one their eyes never blinked–presumably a ball's eyes wouldn't blink because it's an inanimate object.

JC: Precisely. Thank you."The Sun" is another poem that has "after" and I understand that those things with Stuart Ross and Georg–Is Georg Trakl a typo?

SR: No, it isn't. It looks like one, but it isn't. The Georg and the Trakl both look like typos again.

JC: Is he related to Hav?

SR: No, he isn't. They both donated their "e" to the e-collection agency. Georg Trakl was an Austrian poet who died in the early part of the twentieth century.

JC: So you don't know him personally?

SR: I have never met him.

JC: Is the Stuart Ross you mention in "The Sun" the same Stuart Ross as you or is it a different Stuart Ross?

SR: It is the same Stuart Ross as me.

JC: But it is not in this book? It is a different Stuart Ross than was in this book?

SR: It is the same Stuart Ross, but it's a different poem called "The Sun." I have another poem called "The Sun" in another book of mine and it's after a poem called "The Sun" by Georg Trakl, which never appeared in any of my books.

JC: Well, wait a second. So was "The Sun" in the other Stuart Ross poem, in the other Stuart Ross book, after Georg Tarckles?

SR: Yes, it was.

JC: So this one was after...after...?

SR: Yeah, the first one was after a poem by Georg Trakl. This poem is after the poem I wrote after the poem by Georg Trakl. I took a poem by Georg Trakl and I wrote a line after every one of his lines and then I erased his original lines. So what was left standing was my poem, and then I took that poem, which was published around 2003, and I wrote a new line after each of my own lines, nine lines, and then I erased my original lines and what was left standing was *this* poem.

JC: So which was the real poem?

SR: They are all real poems. The poem in this book is the grandchild of the original Georg Trakl poem.

JC: Thank you. When at the end of "The Hill" you say, "This is the place I will die," how do you know? Is it because you killed yourself?

SR: Maybe it's a decision that that's where I'm going to die – but the death hasn't taken place yet. You know, like, "This place here, I think this is where I am going to die."

JC: For real?

SR: The "I" in the poem is perhaps a character, so for that character perhaps, yeah.

JC: Do you know if in fact the "I" in this poem is a character or not?

SR: Since you're going to push me on that, I think that whenever "I" appears in any of my poems, it is a version of me. It is not me or the way I think necessarily, but the place I got my head into in that moment and it probably does have some relation to me.

JC: So if we can follow that logic for just a moment and go back to the previous question. Then the Stuart Ross you are referring to as being "after" in "The Sun" is a different Stuart Ross, in fact, because it is not quite the you that you are.

SR: Well, it is referring to the author there, so it is exactly me. But the "I" in the Stuart Ross poem is some other version of Stuart Ross, and the "I" in this poem, if there is one – There is no "I" in this poem.

JC: We will agree to disagree. Is "The Hill" a very sad poem?

SR: Which "Hill" are you referring to, which page?

JC: "The Hill," on page 29, "The Hill." Is it a very sad poem? Because I find it ends very sadly. As a follow-up question, do you like to put a lot of emotion into your poems?

SR: This is sort of a sad poem; it's a poem about loss. Someone who's just stuck in their tracks. And I don't necessarily put emotion into a poem, I don't know what that means, to put emotion into a poem, but I hope my poems will often evoke some kind of emotion in the reader, but I can't control that. Sometimes I read a poem I find very depressing and the audience laughs, and sometimes I read a poem I think is very funny and the audience goes, "Wow," or different people in the audience think it's serious. So I can't control how someone responds to a poem.

JC: Can you control your poems?

SR: I can control the words and where the lines break, but I can't control how someone reads it.

JC: Can you control how you read it?

SR: No, sometimes I write a poem and I look at it a lot later and suddenly I see a lot of things I didn't think were there before. So I don't think I control it.

JC: How much control do you have?

SR: Of my poems?

JC: Okay.

SR: I choose the words, the lines, the sentences, the breaks. But the poem has its own life. That sounds cliché, but when you write the poem it might have some effect on you and others, and a year later it might have a completely different effect on you and different people. So, I would say I don't have a lot of control over my poems.

JC: I think this will help us get to the bottom of where you put your emotions in your poems, if you do. Is "The Remains" also a sad poem on page 32? Which is sadder: "The Hill" on page 29 or "The Remains" on page 32?

SR: I think "The Remains" is a sadder poem than "The Hill" on page 29, because I think it's just about a person who is completely, completely alone and–

JC: Is that Mark Strand?

SR: No, that is me. Oops, this one is a lot about how I feel. I am an orphan and this poem seems to me to be about an orphan since "my bed holds only me now." It is about a person whose whole life is pared down to just his self. So I think it is a sadder–No, actually they're both really depressing–to me anyways. Some people might find them funny because the poems might be so over-the-top destitute, some people may find that funny. I find them both equally sad.

JC: Does your poetry depress you?

SR: Sometimes my poetry depresses me. There is no hope in this poem, and I don't actually fall into a depression from it, but it makes me feel melancholy, yeah.

JC: Moving on to more pleasant thoughts, at the end of "How Pleasant It Is" you write, "Everything gets mowed flat." Is that a happy ending?

SR: It's possible I was being a little sarcastic writing under that title. That title is the title of a poem by Alice Burdick. I wrote the lines after–

JC: Do you know Alice Burdick?

SR: I *do* know Alice Burdick, yes, she's a great friend. Her title stayed with the poem, but the way I responded to her poem was in pretty depressing imagery. "Everything gets mowed flat" is a pretty bleak ending for sure, but the pleasant title stayed there.

JC: So it is not a happy ending?

SR: I don't find it happy. Did you find it happy?

JC: I think that it could mean that you could get a fresh start.

SR: See, you have an optimistic way of looking at things.

JC: But I don't know for sure. Alice Burdick would know.

SR: She might know...

JC: Say you were reading your poem "In a Forest of Whispers" out loud. Would you read the roman numerals out loud?

SR: I would, yes.

JC: What colour do you stain your lizard in the second part of "In the Forest of Whispers"? And does the lizard mind? And is it inhumane to stain a lizard, in your opinion? And is it inhumane to stain a lizard even in a poem, and does it spread inhumane behaviour?

SR: Yes, it is cruel to stain a lizard. But I like to often just have fun with the language in the poems I write and I don't think of their ethical implications. So I stain my lizard, I don't know if we're actually talking about a lizard–

JC: Are we talking about a lizard in this poem?

SR: It just occurred to me, I have no idea…Maybe lizard is standing for genitals there, I don't know.

JC: Is this a naughty poem?

SR: It could very well be a naughty poem. I guess depending on what, when you read it, is on your mind.

JC: Are we talking about literally staining a lizard?

SR: If that's how you want to read it. The way I wrote this third section of the poem was I went back to the first section and replaced all the nouns and verbs with a verb or noun that came seven or so words before or after that word in my dictionary. So these words are random; there was a bit of curation, but what was interesting to me was what happened by chance.

JC: Is your dictionary an innocent in this whole thing?

SR: All dictionaries are innocent. I made some choices along the way, so I take responsibility.

JC: And what about Charles Simic, then?

SR: He is totally innocent of this because he didn't know what I was doing to his poem and he is a good guy as far as I can tell. I saw him read once in Toronto, but I have never actually spoken with him.

JC: So are you saying that you don't think poems can spread inhumane behaviour? Going back to the last question that I asked?

SR: I don't know how people are going to respond to what I write, and I don't know if I am necessarily responsible for how people respond. So if somebody read the line "stain my lizard" and thought, "Fuck, that would be cool to stain my lizard," and they stain a lizard, I am not responsible for that.

JC: Are poets responsible for anything, if not that?

SR: Poets are responsible for their own actions, but you can't be responsible for someone else's actions; no one can be.

JC: So they shouldn't care about other people's actions?

SR: You can care about them; you are just not responsible. I mean, we are not responsible for how other people act; we can try and influence how other people act, but we are not responsible. We are only responsible for the way we act.

JC: Should you try to influence how people act with lizards?

SR: You know, if I saw someone who was going to stomp on a lizard or was running around staining lizards, then I would probably ask them to reconsider.

JC: In "Earning My Noble Prize for Literature," how can the dogs use dental floss without opposable thumbs? Do their masters have to floss their teeth? As a follow-up question, do you like dogs or cats better?

SR: I prefer most dogs, but it depends on the specific dog and cat. I think there could be a dental floss invented for dogs to use themselves; maybe each end hooks onto one of their nails and so thumbs aren't really necessary for that. You have to expand your mind beyond your own experiences.

JC: So is that the invention then? It is dental floss that hooks onto dog nails? Is that what that line means?

SR: It could also be a floss that is hooked across two walls in a corridor and the dog puts his teeth over it and goes back and forth with his head. I was imagining somebody who was an inventor who could invent that kind of thing, I don't really know the specifics.

JC: Do you think dogs could learn how to floss their teeth?

SR: That's a good question. I think some dogs could if they were going to get a treat for doing it.

JC: I like dogs too. Do you like eating hamburgers?

SR: I haven't eaten a hamburger in about twenty-five years. I'm a vegetarian, but I really enjoy eating good veggie burgers. Is there something about eating burgers in this? Oh yeah, the title of the book has a hamburger in a gallery, I almost forgot.

JC: Okay. In "Study 19," you say you painted paintings. Are you a poet or a painter? It is a bit confusing.

SR: I don't think I've actually ever painted a painting. So that is me using "I" to talk about someone who has painted a painting rather than me specifically. I've made drawings, but I consider myself mostly a poet.

JC: So when you say "I" here you are not referring to any of the Stuart Rosses?

SR: I might be referring to an imaginary Stuart Ross who has a life quite different than my own. Sometimes I see my poems as autobiographical because they contain things that have happened to me or I have done, but that's really, really rare. Usually I see them as sort of emotionally autobiographical because they take on a tone that might reflect my own emotions or my own way of thinking, but the literal things in there aren't actually things I've done or seen.

JC: So is the poem "Study 19" the painting *Study 19,* and did it get advertised?

SR: The poem "Study 19" is a poem that refers to a painting called *Study 19,* and according to the poem, the painting *Study 19* got advertised, but the poem as far as I know has never been advertised.

JC: Did you ever get advertised?

SR: Advertisements have appeared about me; when I've done readings or launched books there have been advertisements that say I'm doing the reading or that my book exists. So in that way I have been advertised, but I haven't been advertised as a human being though.

JC: I understand. Do you really believe that shoes are not clothes? Are socks clothes? Are hats clothes? Is a belt clothes? Eyeglasses? What about garbage bags if it is raining or not raining.

SR: It's just a question I wanted to raise because I wondered if shoes were clothes, and I would say the same thing about glasses. I don't think glasses are clothes, but they are sort of like clothes. If you put a garbage bag over yourself when it is raining, does it become clothes? I think so, but I'm not sure if I've really decided if shoes are clothes.

JC: Do poets get to decide what are clothes and what are not clothes?

SR: No.

JC: Do poets need to help us think about what are clothes and what are not clothes?

SR: They don't need to, but it was something I chose to do in this poem.

JC: Why do you think we want to know what are clothes and what are not clothes?

SR: I'm not saying I thought of this when I wrote the poem, but I'm saying it now: there are certain things that if someone wore, like a stapler as an earring, I would say that it's jewelry, for that person it is jewelry, while another person might use it to staple some papers together. So are things what they are declared to be when they are advertised or are things the things we use them to be? If somebody put a bicycle over himself and walked around with it all the time, would that be considered a piece of his clothing?

JC: I don't think bicycles are clothes. In "Alekhine vs Bogoljubov 1," are you doing an allegory in this poem?

SR: I almost never consciously do allegories.

JC: Are you unconsciously doing an allegory in this poem? In your opinion?

SR: I don't see it that way, but if you interpret it that way I am not going to argue with you.

JC: I don't interpret it that way. In "My Life During a Certain Period," how long was that period of your life?

SR: I'm using a sample of a few days, probably to represent a larger period in my life. The Rosens are mentioned and when I grew up the first 13 years of my life we lived across the street from a family called the Rosens, so I'm probably referring to them, that part of my life ages eight to 13 or so. It's probably about five or six years.

JC: Five or six years? Is it a *bildungsroman* poem or a *kunstlerroman* poem?

SR: Yeah, I don't know what those mean. Something about growing up? Why don't you tell me what those two things mean?

JC: I am asking the questions. Have you ever swam with dolphins?

Don't dolphins look like they are smiling? Are they smiling?

SR: I don't know, someone was telling me dolphins are becoming extinct, so when you look at a photo of a dolphin with that knowledge, it might not look like it's smiling.

JC: What do you know about dolphins?

SR: Almost nothing except that they're supposed to be pretty intelligent.

JC: I have a genre question about the genre of things. What is the difference between one-line poems and one-liners?

SR: A one-liner is a joke and a one-line poem is a poem that lasts only for one line and is not necessarily funny. A good one-line poem should have the qualities of any good poem. A one-liner, you can forget about it once you get to the end when you go "ha, ha."

JC: Are we supposed to memorize poetry?

SR: I don't think we are supposed to, but if you want to, go ahead.

JC: Is it good to?

SR: I don't know what it would achieve to memorize a poem, except maybe if you want to tell a friend a poem you read and you don't have the book handy.

JC: That's good. In the poem "Sonnet," on page forty-sonnet–46, I mean–is the sonnet a real sonnet? What is a sonnet?

SR: I don't think it has all the metric qualifications of a sonnet, but it is 14 lines with a little twist at the end. So I was being a bit playful calling it a sonnet, especially since everything in it is just the name of something. I don't think I could write a Shakespearean sonnet or Petrarchan sonnet.

JC: Is this a Shakespearean sonnet or Petrarchan sonnet?

SR: It is neither; I guess it's a Rossian sonnet.

JC: Is that a real thing?

SR: Nope. You will not find it mentioned in a book.

JC: In the poem "Three Leashes," on page 52, is Rufus a closet homosexual in this poem?

SR: Um, Rufus, is there something–Oh, "I kissed Rufus on the lips and he called me a fag." Well, that is interesting. I had a dog named Rufus when I was a kid, and when I was a kid I was called by other kids "fag" and "homo." So maybe I'm conflating things from that era.

JC: What period of your life was that?

SR: Probably around the same period of my life as in the other poem, age seven to 11 or 12. Although I was probably called a homo and a fag in junior high school because I was a poet, and so it was fashionable to call me a homo or a fag, which were the words used at that time.

JC: Do you think dogs could be fags?

SR: Ah…I don't know anything about that.

JC: Is New Denver a real place?

SR: Yes, it is.

JC: Can you tell me if this poem on New Denver is an homage to New Denver or an elegy for it?

SR: It is not an elegy. An elegy has to be for something that is gone or dying or dead. It is seven small poems about a real place. These are among the only completely "real" poems in the whole book. Everything happened or appeared exactly as it says. They were things that happened on one day when I went kayaking on Slocan Lake.

JC: You saw all of these things?

SR: Well, everything I saw could be interpreted in the way I have depicted it. Like the Valhalla Glacier seemed to be crouching behind these mountains. I don't know if it was actually waiting for its close-up; that's my interpretation.

JC: Did you write these down when you were seeing them?

SR: Yes.

JC: How do you write and kayak at the same time?

SR: I went on a little kayaking trip with this dog Beckham, who sometimes swam and sometimes ran along the shore. Then we stopped on a little pebble-beach outcrop and I wrote the poem there. I actually brought my notebook thinking I might be able to write while I was kayaking, but I'm such a terrible boater and I get such acrophobia that any move I made without the oars I thought I was going to tip over, so that's when I pulled over and did the writing.

JC: Was Beckham on the kayak with you?

SR: He wasn't on the kayak, but a few times he swam alongside the kayak and I was nervous he was going to roll the kayak over, because I'm not a very good kayaker.

JC: Is Beckham behind the dental-floss idea?

SR: No, but hopefully it would benefit Beckham if it were ever invented.

JC: Who do you like better, Beckham or Rufus?

SR: Rufus is a childhood dog of mine and now he is dead. Beckham's alive, so I like Beckham better.

JC: So you like living things better than dead things?

SR: There wouldn't be much purpose in liking Rufus at this point. Beckham is a dog I see every year and I'm fond of him and when I see him in the spring he's excited to see me. If I liked Rufus, it wouldn't matter.

JC: I totally agree with you. In the poem "The Ravine," on page 54, who are you asking this question about the ravine?

SR: I'm probably asking myself. I passed this ravine I used to play in when I was eight or nine years old and wondered if there was any leaf or bark or any plant now that was actually there when I used to play in that ravine. It was the Garthdale ravine in Toronto.

JC: Are you raising that question to yourself Stuart Ross?

SR: I am raising it to myself Stuart Ross, and anyone else who might want to ask such a question if they can relate to it.

JC: A related question that has to do with your poem "Tarjetas Postales," are these postcards being sent to anyone?

SR: Each of these poems is based on a postcard that was sent to Anne Waldman, to whom the poem is dedicated.

JC: You sent these postcards to Anne Waldman?

SR: I didn't send them. I went to a workshop she led, and she threw hundreds of postcards on the table and we each gathered a bunch of postcards we liked and we wrote poems using each postcard as a source, and they were all postcards that had been written to Anne. I didn't send these to her, although I did send her a copy of this poem.

JC: Did she send you a postcard back?

SR: No, she did not.

JC: Did you get to keep her postcards?

SR: No, we gave the postcards all back.

JC: What was the first postcard that you ever wrote?

SR: The first postcard that I ever wrote was to my grandfather, Sam Blatt. He used to go to Miami every winter and I was probably seven or eight and that is my first memory of writing a postcard. It probably said something like "Dear Grandpa, How are you? I am fine, how is the weather there? The weather here is cold. Rufus got hit by a car."

JC: Is that a poem?

SR: What I just said?

JC: That postcard.

SR: No.

JC: Compared to these postcards?

SR: No, but I have a poem that goes almost exactly like that. In fact it was written as an email to a Montrealer named Meaghan and it says: "Dear Meaghan. // How are you?/I am fine. // How is the weather there?/The weather here is rainy," etc. It wasn't a postcard but it had that same tone. I asked myself, could something as banal as this work as a poem?

JC: Can I see it?

SR: Yup.

JC: What is your answer to that question?

SR: What is the question again?

JC: Does that work as a poem?

SR: I don't know yet.

JC: When will you know?

SR: I think I'll look back at this poem here and I see if it works as a poem. More importantly, if people see it in a book and think, "This is weird," then start asking, "What is a poem?" And that is an interesting question to me.

JC: What *is* a poem?

SR: I think it's anything we write and we call a poem. That's what Ted Berrigan says: if you write something and you call it a poem then it is a poem.

JC: Do you know Ted Berrigan?

SR: I do not know him. I've never met Ted Berrigan, but he was a close friend of Ron Padgett and I know Ron.

JC: You seem to refer to people who you know and who you don't know in similar ways. Why is that?

SR: Hmm, I've never considered that.

JC: Do you agree with what the person that you don't know, Ted Berrigan, says is a poem?

SR: I mostly agree with him. Yeah, if someone calls something a poem, it's a poem. It doesn't necessarily mean it's a good poem or a poem that works, but it's a poem if they say it's a poem.

JC: Does it matter who decides?

SR: What matters more is what their argument is for something being a poem or not being a poem. How they can defend it as a poem.

JC: Can you defend "Tarjetas Postales" as a poem?

SR: Yes.

JC: How?

SR: It has the language of poems, like "O what incomparable medicinal value!" That kind of exclamatory language is often found in poetry, and the sequence is almost all imagery. Not that all poetry is imagery, but imagery is an integral part of poetry. Also, they look like poems on the page–sort of like haiku where the syllables haven't been counted, because they're each three lines long. Taken together, they are drawn from a collection of texts all created at different times and in different places and they add up to a kind of a poem collage, something that can be interpreted only by the person who is reading it.

JC: How important is the title or that there is a title in making it a poem?

SR: Not all poems have titles, but most poems have titles, so the fact that it has a title makes it one step closer to being a poem. The title is simply "Tarjetas Postales," a Spanish phrase meaning "postcards."

JC: If you had sent these as postcards, would they still have been poems? If they were never published in a book?

SR: If they were written like this, if they were written out exactly how I have written them out here, I think they would be poems that I sent on the back of postcards, yeah.

JC: Would that hold up in a court of law?

SR: Depends on the judge.

JC: Do you think mailmen should continue to bring mail to people's doors?

SR: Yeah.

JC: Me too, I totally agree. In "A Blob Against the Pointy Moon," do you think that trees have consciousness? I am referring to the line "The tree is aware of the dog's bark."

SR: I don't think that trees have consciousness, but I think it's possible that a tree or a plant can respond to music in some way, but maybe a more physical way. The reverberations of the dog's bark can affect the tree. Or the tree's bark maybe.

JC: What does awareness mean to them?

SR: I think "aware" does suggest consciousness, but just because I put it in a poem doesn't mean I think it's real or possible.

JC: But you believe trees feel?

SR: I think it's possible.

JC: Do you hope it is possible?

SR: No, I guess I probably hope not, because that would be a lot of pain, a lot of trees would feel pain.

JC: They would. At the end of the poem, it makes me think, what would happen if you didn't teach the future the alphabet. What would happen to the future?

SR: You are asking me now and I am considering it at this moment. I'm just looking at the evidence in the poem here. Um, "I teach the future the alphabet." I guess that might suggest I want to help the future learn from my own mistakes or from the mistakes of the past and hope the future is better than the present. I have no fucking idea, really.

JC: Does teaching make you an angel?

SR: Teaching can be a very angelic thing to do. Teaching can be one of the greatest things to do, depending on how one teaches.

JC: Or is it a mosquito, a dragonfly or a bird?

SR: The what?

JC: The wings.

SR: No, I think I'm talking about an angel. A wing on a human makes someone an angel.

JC: In the poem "Normality," on page 63, is the black spot on your collar symbolic? Are any of your poems symbolic?

SR: I never intend symbolism in my poems.

JC: What are symbols? Are they anything?

SR: If people read the line about a black spot on my collar and they interpret it in some way that isn't literal, like what does a black spot mean? Then they might think the black spot is a symbol of whatever they are thinking, and once again I'm not going to disabuse them of that, but I don't intend anything. I never intend symbols.

JC: But do you prefer to read things literally or symbolically?

SR: Pretty much always literally.

JC: Doesn't that go against making poetry deep, though?

SR: I never thought poetry should be deep. It should be something one thinks about, but not necessarily deep. To be honest, I don't know what "deep" means. I don't think poetry works that way. Not the poetry I like anyways.

JC: What are some of the poetries that you like?

SR: I like a lot of different poets' works. Most of the poets we've mentioned, or you've mentioned, are poets I like. I like poetry that doesn't appear to be constructed so that it means something very specific. Like the poem "The Road Not Taken" by Robert Frost is really clever and everything, but to me there is no room to move around. There seems to be a very deliberate intention and there is only one way you can think about it. Unless that's because I've been brainwashed by teachers. I like Ron Padgett's poetry. I like Larry Fagin, and Jaime Forsythe, and David McFadden, and I like Lisa Jarnot's poetry. I like your poetry. I like poets who write things that are filled with enigma, so you might read them differently every time and there's a lot of room to move around, it's not really prescriptive.

JC: What's an enigma?

SR: Um, an unanswered question or a mystery. Something whose very existence you can't explain or whose purpose you can't explain.

JC: That's an enigma?

SR: That's what I would define it as.

JC: In "The Skaters," in the first line of "The Skaters," which reads, "Some funny dogs play tambourines," my same question about dogs flossing seems to apply here, as well.

SR: How can they play a tambourine without opposable thumbs?

JC: I agree.

SR: Like the organ grinder's little monkey with the cymbals, they have little straps that hold those cymbals on their hands. So a tambourine can actually be strapped to a dog's paw.

JC: So that is literally how they can play them?

SR: Yeah, I never really thought of that line: "Some funny dogs play tambourines." It seemed silly and slightly naive; I actually didn't consider the logistics behind it, but I think you could strap a tambourine to a dog's paw.

JC: Literally.

SR: Literally.

JC: On page 65, is the Schubert in this poem the German composer?
SR: The Austrian composer, yes.
JC: You don't actually think you know him? Do you? What is your relationship to Schubert?
SR: I have never met Schubert and I could not name a single one of his pieces of music. I wrote this poem while I was listening to a poem by the American poet John Ashbery and I stole words and phrases from Ashbery's poem and the name Schubert came up and so I threw it into my poem. I've been so intellectually lazy that I haven't even looked up anything about Schubert. I think he wrote sort of sappy classical stuff that I wouldn't like.
JC: You wrote this while you were listening to another poet?
SR: Yeah, I wrote this while listening to the work of a poet read aloud not by that poet.
JC: Who–? This is confusing. Who was reading? You mentioned John Aspine and he was reading, but he wasn't reading. Someone else was reading John Aspine?
SR: Yeah, John Ashbery, the American poet and one of the greatest, certainly most famous, English-language poets alive. He has a poem called "The Skaters" and I was leading a workshop and I had everyone read about half a page of the John Ashbery poem aloud, and while that person was reading, everyone else writes. They can listen, they can *not* listen, they can steal material from that poem, whatever they want. They can use what they are hearing in any way they want while they write their own poem. Then the poem keeps getting passed around the whole room till everyone has read about half a page of it. Some people in the room will have written nine pages of poetry and some will have written 30 to 40 lines or maybe just six lines. It is a method apparently called River of Words, and I interpret that as a river of words going by and whenever you need some words you dip into the river and throw them into your poem. So that is how Schubert ended up in my poem.
JC: So the river is the reader reading the words?

SR: It's the words floating by as each of the readers reads aloud. It's one of my favourite methods of writing.

JC: But you need other people to write then?

SR: Yeah, I imagine I could just put on a recording of John Ashbery reading his poetry or Alice Notley reading her poetry, but I like the idea of it being a communal experience so everyone takes turns reading it, and when they're not reading they're writing.

JC: Was anyone else's poems any good?

SR: Other people who wrote poems while they were listening to the John Ashbery poem? I don't remember the specific moment when I wrote this poem and what other poems were written at that time, but always there are really interesting things happening in other people's poems.

JC: Did it ever happen that you – that two people wrote exactly the same thing? Because you were listening and then you dipped into exactly the same spots in the river of words?

SR: I've never heard of that happening. It's like a chess game – there are so many possibilities that it's impossible to repeat the exact same words twice, but it's interesting that certain words appear in almost everyone's poems. Like the word "landscape" will appear in almost everyone's poem. I don't know why.

JC: What about Schubert?

SR: I don't think anyone else used Schubert.

JC: Does that make you better than them?

SR: Just makes me different than them.

JC: In "The Poem During a Talk by Carla–"

SR: I am just going to point out, you seem to have this preoccupation with me thinking I am better than other people or that poets think they are better than other people. I think it's an interesting issue and I'm bewildered by it.

JC: I find it interesting that you keep coming back to that, too. In "Poem During a Talk by Carla Harryman," did you write this during a talk by Carla Harryman or did it happen during that talk?

SR: I wrote this during a talk by Carla Harryman in Montreal, at a little French bookstore in the Plateau, Le Port de Tête. I was so excited about Carla Harryman talking because I love so many of her poems, but it was her reading some fucking incomprehensible mind-numbing theoretical stuff and the only way I could keep myself from screaming or walking out was to write a poem. So I will say that I just didn't understand it, I was just too stupid for her talk–I was not better than anyone else there.
JC: But you wrote poetry while you were listening to her talk? Are you writing poetry right now while you are listening to me talk?
SR: No.
JC: Isn't it kind of rude to write poetry when someone is talking?
SR: I was in the back row and I tried to be as discreet as possible. I don't think anyone saw me and if anyone saw me they'd probably just think I was taking notes. There were other people taking notes, so maybe there were other people writing poems.
JC: So you were writing poetry to pretend you were taking notes? Kind of?
SR: I was writing poetry to keep myself interested and I thought it was too rude to just get up and leave. Also I was in a bookstore and I wanted to do some shopping when the talk was over. It wasn't to make people think I was taking notes.
JC: In the poem "Did You Believe Me?" on page 69, you ask, "Did you believe me?" Is this poem about the truth, imagination or lies, and did you write it because you had been hurt by lies? And do you believe that honesty is possible? What about the truth?
SR: "Did You Believe Me?" was written while I was listening to a book-length poem called "What" by Ron Silliman; people around the table were reading it and passing it around.
JC: Was Ron Silverman there?
SR: Silliman. He was not there, although he's alive and I've seen him once although I've never met him, I do not know him. I might've been introduced to him if he was there, but no, he was not there, and now

I've forgotten all of the other questions.

JC: Is this poem about truth, imagination or lies?

SR: I tend to not write poems that are *about* something, I don't really think about the about-ness when I think of poems. I also don't remember my poems, so when you ask me I usually have to look at it and read it really quickly. "I'm just kidding. Did you believe me?" Oh, so maybe it's about imagination and maybe it's about lying. Is a poem a lie? I can write any crap I want in a poem and did you believe me? Because a lot of people say that poetry is about truths, and these weren't things I was thinking of when I was writing the poem, but I'm thinking about them as I look at the poem. People say poetry is a way of getting to truth, or a way of expressing beauty, and I don't believe any of those things, but here I am saying all this shit and then saying, "Did you believe me?"

JC: So it is not about the truth, but imagination and lying?

SR: If people read things in a poem, do they think it's truth because it's in a poem? And yet it is just me writing some shit.

JC: So as I asked earlier, it seems like you didn't answer it. Did you write it because you have been hurt by lies?

SR: Um...no.

JC: Do you believe that honesty is possible?

SR: I don't think that a piece of art has to be honest, but I think the creation of it has to be honest in some way.

JC: So you have to make it honestly, but the poem that you make doesn't have to be honest?

SR: I could live with that.

JC: Well, what about the truth then? If you make it honestly, then are you creating the truth with your poem?

SR: No, I don't believe that. I don't believe poems are about truths, necessarily.

JC: Are they about lies?

SR: I don't think they are *about* lies; I think they might *contain* lies and they might contain truths, but I don't think they are about either of those things necessarily. Yet, this poem ends as it says, "Did you believe me? Did you believe me?" and we don't go back to that at all so...either what the poem is "about" disappears or it is part of a way to read the rest of the poem with that in mind. I'm just suggesting this as if I was reading a poem by someone else.

JC: Like how important is it for your reader to believe your poems? Or *how* should they believe your poems?

SR: I think they should just go along with a poem and respond in any way they want to respond. If the poem doesn't interest them or my writing doesn't interest them, then they can read Rod McKuen or Carmine Starnino.

JC: Like are we supposed to believe that "A horse taught an enthusiastic/class on how to snort?"

SR: You're not *supposed* to believe it, but I think it's a pretty funny idea. That's why I wrote it.

JC: So if we are not supposed to believe it, even though you asked if we believe you–which suggests that whether or not we believed you is important–what are we supposed to do with that?

SR: You can do whatever you want with it. Just because I said "Do you believe me?" that doesn't prescribe anything. "Hey do you believe me? I just say this shit" is implied, so people can just go on and read this in any way they want without looking for truths or anything. When I started reading John Ashbery I had a lot of trouble. I tried *The Tennis Court Oath* and *Self-Portrait in a Convex Mirror* and I felt like I was missing something. I felt really stupid trying to read John Ashbery. And then I read an interview with John Ashbery who said, to the best of my recollection, he didn't *mean* anything in his poems–he just wrote to amuse people. Then I read some newer books by Ashbery, like *Chinese Whispers* and *Flow Chart,* and I read them like I was looking at an abstract painting–I responded how I might respond in a visceral or surface way to a painting. I was then freed to read his poetry, and now I go back and I love those old books of his because I found it liberating to know I could respond in any way I felt like responding, emotionally or viscerally or laughing at things or being bewildered by things. It was okay to just be bewildered.

JC: Speaking of love, because you said you loved those John Ashbery poems, is love a feeling? Or is it just chemicals? And do you believe in love?

SR: I haven't thought about whether love is a feeling or if it's just chemicals. I imagine that there is some of both mixed in. I know that it's possible with depression, so it makes sense it might be possible with love. Do I believe in love? Um…

JC: Because it sounds like it is more important that you *love* John Ashbery than that you *understand* John Ashbery. So it seems like you believe in love more than you believe in understanding.

SR: Well, I would say that's a misinterpretation of what I said. It is not more important that I love him than that I understand him. I love John Ashbery because I was freed from what I thought was an obligation to understand him and I can respond to him in ways that are much more visceral and instinctual, so therefore I mostly love his poetry. As for love, I don't know if I believe in it or not because I don't know what it would mean to believe in love.

JC: On page 74 the poem has the same title as the section of the book "Dick TV." Is "Dick TV" dirty? Is it a dirty poem?

SR: I think Dick Cheney, who is the Dick of the poem, is dirty, filthy, disgusting and a horrific human being. I like the fact that his name is the same pejorative word that we use to call someone a dick.

JC: Why do you think that it is also what we call private detectives?

SR: I don't know. I was going to say that it comes out of Dick Tracy, but it's probably the other way around and Dick Tracy comes out of dick… No idea.

JC: But dick is sort of like a lizard here, you are saying?

SR: Dick Cheney himself might be one of those amphibious creatures possibly from another planet.

JC: In "Melophanologo," you have a line that says, "Consciousness is only the memory of consciousness." Do humans have a special kind of memory? Don't dogs have memories too? What is the difference?
SR: I don't even know why you would ask this in relation to this poem...
JC: Well, because I don't think dogs can remember being conscious as far as I can tell from the dogs that I have known – Finnick, Haika, Sparky, Dusty, Patches, Romeo...I don't think so.
SR: So you're saying that dogs can be conscious or have a consciousness, but my definition of consciousness is wrong because dogs don't have memories?
JC: No, I am asking if humans have a special kind of memory, because you are saying that consciousness is only a memory of consciousness. Yet, I don't think that dogs have a memory of consciousness, or are you saying that they do?
SR: I am not saying anything about dogs in this poem, which was also written in the Anne Waldman workshop, and I no longer remember what the word "melophanologo" means. We were trying to demonstrate six different things, one with each of these lines, and those things somehow added up to "Melophanologo." It's amazing I can write a poem and not even know what the title means anymore and still stand by the poem. I am evading your question here obviously.
JC: Do humans have a special kind of memory?
SR: I suspect they do, but I don't know. I assume that dogs' memory is a lot more of an instinctual thing, they have associations and they can't go and just think about when they were a three-year-old puppy. But I don't know for sure.
JC: Me neither, but you define consciousness in this poem and you say it is only the memory of consciousness. Is that what you think?
SR: I think it is a possibility.
JC: Do you think it refers to the L-O part of the title?
SR: Yeah, probably does. Do you know what it means?

JC: Maybe it means loss.

SR: Loss?

JC: In "Fast Food," it made me wonder if you eat fast food?

SR: Very, very rarely. I used to eat it more frequently, but almost never now.

JC: What do you like better: salt or sugar?

SR: Salt.

JC: In "Self-Portrait with a Penny," as a Jew do you find it difficult to pick up a penny when you see one?

SR: Yes, if anyone sees me. If I feel like anyone might see me, then yes.

JC: Do you still pick up pennies anyways?

SR: It's harder to find pennies now, but I passed a dime on the ground today and I didn't stoop to pick it up, and when I say stoop I mean physically.

JC: Returning to pennies, why would you pick up a penny now, because you know pennies are no longer worth anything?

SR: Yes, I don't necessarily stoop to pick up pennies myself. I am not necessarily the person speaking in this poem. I don't have a lot of money now, but when I had a lot less money and money was much harder to come by, seeing a penny, nickel or a dime on the ground, and you see one almost every day, you know this must add up to something. Maybe five bucks a year, fifteen bucks, I don't know, but I thought that was sort of neat, especially back when you could buy something with a dime. Finding a dime on the ground you could buy an *Archie* comic.

JC: You said earlier that as a Jew you find it difficult to pick up a penny when you see one. Why is that?

SR: Um, because of the stereotype of Jews being money-grubbing, money-obsessed people.

JC: Do you care what people think about you?

SR: Yes.

JC: In "Elegy," on page 78, I noticed that some of your poems were very short.

SR: Yes, some of my poems are very short, I agree.

JC: On page 80 there is a poem called "Political Poem." Isn't all poetry political?

SR: I think all poetry is political in some way insofar as almost everything is political if you look at the context that something occurs in and the effect it might have. I don't know if all poems are political poems, but there could be a political way of looking at a poem or reading politics into a poem.

JC: Do you believe there is even something like Canadian political poetry?

SR: I don't understand your question.

JC: Do you believe in Canadian political poetry?

SR: Um, a poem that contains politics that is by a Canadian? Then yes, I think that Canadians can write poems that have political readings to them or have politics in them.

JC: But poems don't influence people?

SR: Um, did I –

JC: Getting back to the lizard and painting the lizard. We don't care what the poems do, because you are not responsible for someone painting a lizard, you said.

SR: Wow. I think some people might be influenced by a poem.

JC: Do you try to influence people with your poetry?

SR: No, I try to catch their interest.

JC: So this is not a political poem.

SR: It says in the first line that this is a political poem, yet I also said that my poems don't necessarily have to speak truths. But this poem is, in fact, largely about politics.

JC: So a political poem can be about politics but not influence people to a particular political opinion.

SR: Yes.

JC: The poem "Crunch" made me think about why do you think it is called Cap'n Crunch and why not Major Crunch or General Crunch?

SR: I think it was just an issue of alliteration.

JC: Do you like alliteration?

SR: I don't like alliteration in contemporary poetry because I think it distracts and takes you out of the poem and it seems to be a self-consciously clever thing to do and I am not usually a big fan of self-conscious cleverness.

JC: Do you believe in sound in poetry?

SR: There is sound in poetry; any poetry has sound in it.

JC: Do you like to read out loud?

SR: I like to read poetry that I like out loud.

JC: Is it different than reading it without sound?

SR: In some ways, when you read it in your head, you hear it in your head, still. Yet I definitely think that when you read a poem out loud you hear a lot of things you can't notice, or it would be harder to notice, if you were reading it in your head.

JC: In the poem "Beans," on page 83, do beans refer to something?

SR: Yeah, the little round things like those in the chili I was just eating. Yeah, beans are beans.

JC: So beans are referring to beans.

SR: In my mind, the beans refer to beans. I literally just meant beans – black beans, kidney beans.

JC: Have beans ever appeared in poetry before?

SR: I can't think offhand of any poems about beans, but I bet there are a ton of poems that contain bean references, and I am sure there are a lot of Latin American poems that do. Also, there is *Bean Spasms* by Ron Padgett, Ted Berrigan and Joe Brainard. That's another place that beans have appeared in poems.

JC: In your poem "Unt

itled," on page 90, will your poem always be untitled?

SR: I can't see me or someone else giving this poem a title.

JC: I noticed that you actually wrote the title in two words, "Unt" and "itled."

SR: I have absolutely no reason for having done that, except that I did write the poems themselves first. So when I went back to write the title, I was perhaps playing a little joke on the ridiculousness of things like "eyegl asses" or "eye glasses." Also it interested me to have a title of a poem that had to appear on two lines because usually a title appears on one line, unless it's a really long title that spills over onto a second line.

JC: On page 92 and subsequently I noticed that the size of the letters get bigger here. Is this to fill up more space? And it also made me think that I should ask if this is a good use of paper?

SR: If I was a bestselling author and this book was going to sell 10 million copies, then it would be a horrible use of paper, but seeing that I'm expecting the book to sell between 300 and 500 copies, I don't think it's that big a deal. If every poet wrote poems like this then it might be a terrible waste of paper. I liked the idea of one word taking control of the entire field of a page and the effect that has. I made the font bigger because I didn't want it to look like you have a page and you have a little piece of ant shit or something on the page and you have to squint to look at it. I wanted the word to command the page without it being giant. I thought it would be more pleasing-looking on the page if it was larger.

JC: So this is part of "Unt
itled"?

SR: No, that's an interesting question and it actually reminds me also why I made those poems larger. In my mind they're separate poems and they have no titles, but to put "Untitled" at the top of each of them would defeat the purpose of having this poem that commands the page. The one word is the only thing on the page, so maybe this was the intention as well – with a different-size lettering it would clearly be a new poem. If you look at the Contents page, all these appear as if the title of this one is "Pretendd" and the title of this one is "Sallowe'en," so it is clear they are separate poems.

JC: So that is the title and the poem?

SR: I am referring to the poem by the single word that appears in the poem. It is more of an identifier, but it is not the title of the poem.
JC: How long does it take you to write a one-word poem?
SR: Um, I think there are about five or six of them here and it probably took me about 10 or 12 minutes to write them. I wrote a few others that I abandoned.
JC: Ten or 12 minutes per poem?
SR: For the whole batch of them; I wrote them in one of my workshops.
JC: So two minutes per poem?
SR: You know, some of the poems came to me instantly, like the idea of putting an extra "d" on "pretend," it sort of just popped into my mind pretty quickly, and some of them I worked on for a while. As I said, in that 10 or 12 minutes I actually wrote more poems than are here, but I didn't think they all worked.
JC: I understand. When you say more poems, do you mean more words?
SR: More one-word poems.
JC: So how many total did you write in 12 minutes? I am just trying to get the exact average per minute of writing a poem.
SR: About a minute and a half?
JC: I can't do that math. "WhyCrest Avenue the Second." Is "WhyCrest Avenue" autobiographical?
SR: I lived on Wychcrest Avenue, as we pronounced it, instead of WhyCrest–I lived on that street for 11 or 12 years, near downtown Toronto. In "Wychcrest Avenue I," those were things I actually saw. It was during a workshop I led in minimalist poetry and I told everyone in the workshop to go outside and walk around and write poems about very specific small things we see that most people don't notice. Then, in "Wychcrest II," I sort of did some mixing and matching from the "Wychcrest I" poems to create new things that I didn't see. Like I didn't see a rectangular white red dog, for example.
JC: So it is autobiographical?
SR: It's sort of a mash-up of autobiographical poems in "Wychcrest II."

JC: Is a double sonnet twice as good as a single sonnet?

SR: It is just twice as long. It is not a matter of quality; it is a matter of length.

JC: I noticed on page 107 you have one word on the page, but it is smaller than the other poems. So is this not a poem and just a part of another poem and that's why it is smaller?

SR: Yeah, it's one of a sequence of poems that make up the poem called "Then:." Because I don't want the word "polio" to have any more meaning or weight than any of the other words in the poem, it appears on a page by itself in the regular font size.

JC: How are we supposed to read the word "polio"? Is it suppose to be in an angry voice or a happy voice or...How do we actually read the word out loud?

SR: I don't want to prescribe how people should read that word. I like the idea of reading this poem as a sequence of poems being read out loud and I would be really interested in hearing how people read them, but I don't want to tell them *how* to read them. That would be like telling people how to react to poems, which I would never do.

JC: Do you care how people react to your poems?

SR: I am interested, but I don't care in the sense that I hope they react to it in a certain way.

JC: And yet you care how people react to your actions?

SR: Yeah, some of my actions, yeah. Are you saying that in terms of my caring about how people think about me?

JC: Like picking up the penny.

SR: Yeah...

JC: So in a way, is poetry a way for you to do things without caring about what people think about you?

SR: I don't write poems so that I can do something by which people won't judge me. If that is what you are asking.

JC: That's interesting. Finally, your poem "Spelling" made me wonder if you think you need to know how to spell to be a poet?

SR: I think you need to know how to spell because you are communicating certain words, and if you are writing words that people can't make out, what is that word then...Like you spelling my name Roth instead of Ross, so–

JC: *Touché.*

SR:–spelling is important, but if you make an occasional spelling error and a friend or editor helps you, then that's good, but I think it's important to know how to spell.

JC: Because bill bissett does not really know how to spell, it seems to me, having seen some of his poems. Yet he is a Canadian poet.

SR: I don't know if what you see on the page in a bill bissett book is an indicator of whether or not he knows how to spell. I think he is deliberately not wanting to follow the rules of spelling, but he might know exactly how to spell the words.

JC: So you don't have to spell correctly to be a poet, but you have to know how to spell, you are saying?

SR: Yeah.

JC: Do you believe in Canadian spelling?

SR: That's an amazing question. I'm a believer in using the Canadian spelling because it sets us apart from the United States, and anything that sets us apart I think is good. Also there's something really ugly about the word "cigarette" without the extra "te" at the end. I wouldn't say that I believe in it, as in that it's something that will save us.

JC: So it is more like you do it.

SR: I do it.

JC: You do Canadian spelling.

SR: I do Canadian spelling.

JC: He sure does do it. Thank you very much, Stuart Ross.

SR: This has been excruciating.

January 18, 2015, Montreal

NOTES

"The Continuing Saga of the Wind" and "Love" were written during "A Wave" by John Ashbery. "A Blob Against the Pointy Moon" might have been written during "A System" by Ashbery but "Towards the Future" certainly was. Part I of "The Skaters" was written during "The Skaters" by Ashbery. "Confetti" during Ashbery's "Flow Chart." "Lesion of Superheroes" during "The Secret Life of Ford Madox Ford," by Ted Berrigan. "Buildings, Winter" during Bernadette Mayer's "A Month of Noons." "Normality" and "Did You Believe Me?" during Ron Silliman's "What." "Poem During a Talk by Carla Harryman" during just such a talk at Le Port de Tête in Montreal, March 18, 2013.

Wychcrest Avenue is a street northwest of Toronto's Annex neighbourhood; I lived in a housing co-op there for over a decade, and lead most of my Toronto writing workshops there. Most of the poems in this book were written in my own workshops, in Toronto, Vancouver and New Denver.

"Dick TV," "Melophanologo" and "Tarjetas Postales" were written during a wonderful workshop given by Anne Waldman for the Toronto New School of Writing in 2011.

My mother took me to see Claes Oldenburg's "Floor Burger" at the Art Gallery of Ontario when I was eight or nine years old. It was a transformative experience and possibly responsible for the nature of my poetry. The giant burger recently underwent life-saving surgery.

"Self-Portrait with a Penny" appears in a musical setting on the 2014 CD *Juan Lonely Night,* by the noise trio Donkey Lopez, of which I am a member. In fact, snippets and phrases from several other poems herein have crept into our improvs. Visit donkeylopez.com.

Christine Miscione contributed a few words to "Abecedarium Apology," and Caroline Szpak supplied the title "Shoes Are Not Clothes." The title for "The Ravine" comes from Paul Quarrington's last published novel, which has sat at my bedside for several years.

One of my great poetry heroes, Ron Padgett, translated a collection of poems by the Chinese poet Yu Jian. It's called *Flash Cards* (Zephyr, 2010). I did not reference Ron's translations when I wrote my own.

"Morning Farmer" is from a German translation of a poem by Ted Berrigan in *Guillaume Apollinaire Ist Tot. Und Anderes* (März Verlag, 1970).

Chess grandmaster Alexander Alekhine wrote a series of anti-Semitic articles in a French Nazi newspaper during the 1940s, in which he posited that Jews were destroying chess by, basically, making it tedious and sapping it of its artistry. His sometime opponent over the board, Efim Bogoljubov, may or may not have been a member of the Nazi Party; there is much debate. He once said, "When I am White I win because I am White. When I am Black I win because I am Bogoljubov."

The one-word poems in the Wychcrest Avenue section owe their very existence, of course, to Aram Saroyan. Inspiration for other of the minimalist poems comes from Nelson Ball.

For the one-line poems, I have the late Kenneth Koch and the late Joe Brainard to thank.

I have not yet won the Nobel Prize for Literature. I mean I could, but I just don't feel like trying that hard.

ACKNOWLEDGEMENTS

Some of these poems have previously appeared – often in earlier versions – in chapbooks and leaflets, and journals online and physical.

"Adventures in Bruxism" on *Cosmonauts Avenue.*

"Poem During a Talk by Carla Harryman," "The Only Synagogue," "The Mirror," "Study 19," "Three Leashes" and "Sonnet [First Men in the Moon.]" in the Bookthug chapbook *In In My Dream.*

"One Eye" and "4 Tiny Poems I Wrote on March 15, 2014" in *Fell Swoop.*

"Beans" and "Earning My Nobel Prize for Literature" in *Event.*

"Self-Portrait with a Penny" in *Matrix.*

"Everybody Had Lost Track of Time," "Normality" and "Crunch" in *Stone the Crows*!

"How Pleasant It Is" in *illiterature.*

"Buildings, Winter," "Melophanologo," "And Boing," "Did You Believe Me?" and "Sonnet [Stranger in a Strange Land.]" on *Experiment-O.*

"Abecedarium Apology," "The Ravine," "The Sun," "Elegy," "Sonnet [Bye Bye Birdie.]" and "Angry Forester" in the Puddles of Sky Press chapbook *Nice Haircut, Fiddlehead.*

"Poem During a Talk by Carla Harryman" on *Poetryeater.*

"Curtains" on *Cordite.*

"Dick TV" in *Gargoyle.*

"4 Tiny Poems I Wrote on March 15, 2014," "My Life During a Certain Period," "The Mirror," "Shoes Are Not Clothes" and "Study 19" as Proper Tales Press leaflets.

Thanks to all the editors involved for their interest in my work.

I am also enormously grateful to the citizens of Ontario, who funnelled me much-needed funds through two excellent Ontario Arts Council programmes meant to buy writers time to write—Writers' Reserve and Writers' Works in Progress. We're so fortunate to have the OAC, and nobody better mess with it.

To too many friends to mention: thank you for the encouragement and support. Nick Papaxanthos: thanks for the comments on a contraband copy of this MS.

Terry Taylor: thank you for the loan of Beckham and the kayak. And for New Denver.

To those who have taken my workshops: thank you for working in the laboratory with me.

To Laurie Siblock, thanks for the collaboration, the unrelenting enthusiasm and the heart of creativity.

And, finally, thanks to Jason Camlot for being such a supportive, patient, risk-taking and provocative editor.

Stuart Ross published his first literary pamphlet on the photocopier in his dad's office one night in 1979. Through the 1980s, he stood on Toronto's Yonge Street wearing signs like "Writer Going To Hell," selling over 7,000 chapbooks. He is the author of more than 15 books of fiction, poetry and essays, including *Our Days in Vaudeville* (Mansfield Press), collaborations with 29 poets from across Canada. *You Exist. Details Follow.* (Anvil Press, 2012) won the only prize given to an anglophone writer in 2013 by l'Académie de la vie littéraire au tournant du 21e siècle. Stuart's many chapbooks include three released in 2014–*Nice Haircut, Fiddlehead* (Puddles of Sky Press), *A Pretty Good Year* (Nose in Book Publishing) and *In In My Dream* (BookThug)–and others from Room 3O2 Books, The Front Press, Apt. 9 Press, Silver Birch Press, Pink Dog Press and his own Proper Tales Press, which he launched 36 years ago. He is co-translator of *My Planet of Kites,* by Marie-Ève Comtois (Mansfield Press, 2015). Stuart is a member of the improvisational noise trio Donkey Lopez, whose CDs include *Juan Lonely Night* and *Working Class Burro.* He is a founding member of the Meet the Presses collective and has his own imprint, "a stuart ross book," at Mansfield Press. Stuart lives in Cobourg, Ontario, and blogs at bloggamooga.blogspot.ca.